WILD
SUBURBIA

WILD SUBURBIA

LEARNING TO GARDEN WITH NATIVE PLANTS

BARBARA EISENSTEIN

To Emiko & Sean,
Be Wild!
Barbara Eisenstein

Heyday, Berkeley, California

*Dedicated to the memory of
my mother, who taught me
the true spirit of gardening*

This project was made possible in part by a generous grant from
the Stanley Smith Horticultural Trust.

Library of Congress Cataloging-in-Publication Data

Names: Eisenstein, Barbara, author.
Title: Wild suburbia : learning to garden with native plants / Barbara Eisenstein.
Other titles: Learning to garden with native plants
Description: Berkeley, CA : Heyday, [2016]
Identifiers: LCCN 2016001540 | ISBN 9781597143639 (pbk. : alk. paper)
Subjects: LCSH: Native plant gardening--California. | Endemic
  plants—California.
Classification: LCC SB439.24.C2 E37 2016 | DDC 635.9/67609794—dc23
LC record available at http://lccn.loc.gov/2016001540

Cover Art: Barbara Eisenstein
Cover Design: Ashley Ingram
Photos: All photos, except those on page 47, by Barbara Eisenstein
Interior Design/Typesetting: Leigh McLellan Design

Orders, inquiries, and correspondence should be addressed to:
  Heyday
  P.O. Box 9145, Berkeley, CA 94709
  (510) 549-3564, Fax (510) 549-1889
  www.heydaybooks.com

Printed in East Peoria, IL, by Versa Press, Inc.

10 9 8 7 6 5 4 3 2 1

CONTENTS

PREFACE

IF YOU'VE PICKED up this book, presumably you are curious about gardening with native plants. Perhaps you admire your neighbor's garden with its colorful California poppies and spicy-scented sages. Perhaps you are looking to be more drought conscious and save on your water bill by transforming your green lawn into a landscape better suited to California's dry climate. Perhaps you share scientists' growing concerns about endemic wildlife and want to do your part to offer refuge to the bustling birds, butterflies, bees, and lizards in your community. Perhaps you are uneasy about the poisons and pesticides that go into green lawns and nonnative gardens and want to be more in tune with the natural landscape and its seasons, rhythms, and native species. Perhaps you already know a bit and want to learn more.

In all of these cases, this book is for you! And if you need more convincing about the advantages of gardening with native species, you will find plenty in the pages that follow. There are many good books on the market about native gardening in California, but when I first undertook my own California native garden, I couldn't find one that addressed the beginning native gardener, offered a personal perspective, emphasized the transition from green lawn to native garden (and what's required for its ongoing maintenance), and shared common pitfalls. This is my attempt to fill that gap.

For me the journey to this wild suburbia began in a new house, in a new part of the country. Moving from the East Coast to the West, I felt disoriented and homesick. I missed the lush green summers, vibrant fall foliage, and the rejuvenating spring flowers, if not the cold winters. I wanted to feel at home in hot, dry Southern California. I wanted to understand the seasons that were barely noticeable in their subtlety.

It was through gardening that I learned to appreciate and love a world of brown and gray, where rain, if it comes at all, is sparse and sequestered into less than half the year. The unusual pattern of winter rains and dry summer heat that gives us subdued colors through much of the year is also responsible for the spectacular burst of color during our spring wildflower season. I still miss the lush green of the East Coast, but I have come to understand and love our own seasons and the remarkable ways that plants and animals have adapted to life here. Wherever you live, you too can feel more at home if you understand and accept the natural conditions around you.

Join me on this journey from an artificial and controlled suburbia to a wild and fun landscape just outside the door. Although the Mediterranean climate of coastal California requires gardening practices that differ from those used in most of the rest of the world, the general concepts presented here apply wherever you put trowel to soil.

· · ·

This book is divided into six sections: Before You Start, Get to Know Your Yard, Formulate Your Plan, Learn about Native Plants, Create Your Garden, and Keep Your Garden Alive. Within each section, I include stories of my own wild suburbia and share practical information on habitat gardening with native plants. In an effort to make the book helpful to both novices and expert gardeners, I use common names for plants in the text. At the end of the book you will find plants listed with both their common and botanical names. (See Resources, page 202.)

Much of what I know about gardening with native plants comes from my work at Rancho Santa Ana Botanic Garden, the largest botanical garden dedicated to California native plants. With a heightened awareness of the need to conserve water, the garden acquired funding from the Metropolitan Water District of Southern California (MWD) to develop a program to facilitate the successful use of water-wise native plants in residential and public gardens. The campaign disseminated information through a dedicated telephone hotline, e-mails, the garden's website, publications, community-education classes, and other outreach venues. Running this program gave me access to excellent

questions from gardeners near and far, as well as reliable answers from
my knowledgeable colleagues at the garden.

At the same time, I also founded a community stewardship program in a local nature park. In 2004 a three-acre habitat park opened
in South Pasadena, and in the following years, weeds threatened to
overwhelm the native plantings. With city support, I started Friends
of South Pasadena Nature Park, and for the past ten years, I have held
monthly cleanups, park tours, planting parties, and other educational
events. Volunteers including students, scouts, adults, and seniors have
removed invasive weeds, planted natives, grown wildflowers, and
nurtured the new additions. We have watched native plants survive
under the harshest conditions, and tried many strategies to reduce
the onslaught of nonnative, invasive weeds. A once degraded, weedy
lot has gradually become a vibrant habitat of local sage scrub and
woodland plants.

The information I learned during these efforts has also been put to
the test in my own garden, where I have gradually replaced lawn and
other water-thirsty, nonnative plants with more appropriate California
natives. I have made plenty of mistakes, and I hope this book presents
them honestly so others can learn from my errors.

I have learned much from these gardening experiences, but ex-
changing ideas with other gardeners, both professionals and hobbyists, has been the most informative. Not only is there much to share,
but gardeners make good friends.

This book would not have been possible without the help, friend-
ship, and support of many people. I would like to thank Ellen Mackey
for introducing me to the "wilds" of Los Angeles when I first arrived
on the West Coast. Our adventures while mapping vegetation along
the Los Angeles River taught me much about my new home, its unfor-
tunate present condition, and its great potential.

Thanks also go to the following people who taught me about
plants, and much more. Bart O'Brien, my closest mentor, generously
shared his immense knowledge of the horticultural use of California
plants, while setting an example of precision and excellence. Susan
Jett's expertise, enthusiasm, and kindness broadened my understand-

ing and guided me through many plant sales and garden events. Dave Lannom gave me a strong foundation in horticulture, and a better perspective on life, as he reminded my classmates and me, "It's just a plant. If you make a mistake, it won't get mad. At worst, it will die."

I am grateful to more people than I can list for sharing their knowledge of plants and the environment, along with a strong desire to do the right thing. Among them are: Carol Bornstein, Helena Bowman, Mike Evans, Naomi Fraga, Lorrae Fuentes, the late Dorothy Green, Emily Green, Mike Letteriello, Lucinda McDade, Joan McGuire, Claire Robinson, Richard Schneider, Lili Singer, Helen Smisko, Sula Vanderplank, Michael Wall, the late Scott Wilson, and Linda Worlow.

I am also indebted to the many volunteers whose generosity gave me confidence in the future of our world. Their tenacity is reflected in the accomplishments of organizations including: Amigos de los Rios, the Arroyo Seco Foundation, the California Native Plant Society, the Council for Watershed Health, Friends of South Pasadena Nature Park, North East Trees, Rancho Santa Ana Botanic Garden, the Theodore Payne Foundation, SPROUTS Environmental Trust (India), Tree of Life Nursery, and TreePeople.

The seeds for this book surely were planted at Rancho Santa Ana Botanic Garden. Many of the photographs that illustrate the beauty of California native plant gardens were taken there, and the plant lists and information on plant care resulted from my collaboration with that organization. I must also thank my publisher, Heyday, and its encouraging and patient editors, Gayle Wattawa and Lisa K. Marietta. Their professional guidance has immeasurably improved this book; nevertheless, any errors or inaccuracies are mine and mine alone.

Of course, the book would never have come to be without the love, tolerance, and support of my family. Thanks go to my kids, who put up with me while I practiced Latin by naming plants everywhere we went, and I must also mention the late Milo, my dog, mascot, and gardening buddy. Most importantly, I owe my deepest gratitude to my husband, whose love, confidence, and encouragement helped me continue even when I was convinced there was no reason to.

GARDEN INTERLUDE: YOU ARE IN VIOLATION

t is April Fools' Day. I am standing at my rather imposing front door with a rather imposing local television reporter. The long strip between the sidewalk and street on the east side of my house is ablaze with wildflowers. The orange poppies, blue globe gilias, and azure ceanothus spill over their borders. The sidewalk garden is to be featured in a native plant garden tour in a few days, and this television reporter is about to interview me for a local news spot about the tour. Just as we are talking, my dog, Milo, whose only household responsibility is to be a living doorbell, starts barking like mad at the mail carrier who has just stopped by. Without thinking, I open the door, pull in the mail, and flip through it quickly. The neatly addressed, official-looking envelope from my city has an ominous feel. With the reporter standing there I tear it open and come face-to-face with a letter informing me that the city "received a report of vegetation growing in the parkway adjacent to [our] home obstructing the public sidewalk in

A honeybee carrying pollen hovers over a California poppy.

California poppies bloom in my parkway garden each spring.

violation of blah, blah, blah. We suggest"—suggest!—"you cut down the vegetation to no higher than twelve inches."

So how did I change from being a law-abiding citizen with a conformist yard dominated by green lawn to a flagrant violator of city code? How did this ordinary yard become home and restaurant for bright-yellow butterflies, orange dragonflies, and red-throated hummingbirds? When did lizards start lurking in the compost bin, resting up before doing battle with large iridescent beetles? When did bright-green spiders start setting up webs to capture and eat stinging bees? Who invited robber flies to hunt for prey into which they would inject toxin, turning their insides into a nutritious milkshake? This book is the story of the transformation of an everyday, mild-mannered yard into a wild suburbia.

Bigleaf crownbeard, an endangered species, flowers among native grasses in my parkway.

BEFORE YOU START

THERE ARE MANY rewards awaiting those who wish to create a wild garden of native plants. In this section, you will learn how to begin the process. We start with a look at the many ways in which native plants make ideal garden environments, then we move to an overview of different approaches to creating a native garden, and we end with a short discussion about the best times to plant. Take out a pencil and clipboard and be prepared to not only learn about the many benefits of native gardening but to also ask yourself incisive questions about what you want and what will work in your yard.

WHY GARDEN WITH NATIVE PLANTS?

You may be wondering why there's so much buzz about gardening with native plants. Considering the increasing concern over global climate change and drought, you might suspect the main reason is to replace water-thirsty lawn with plants that only need a sip now and then. There are many nonnative plants that fill this need, however, so why should we choose native plants instead? Because native plants go

Desert sand verbena.

beyond solving a single problem. Below I list a few of the many benefits to growing this diverse group of plants, but the primary reason I use them is because they are beautiful. If you don't already think so yourself, I hope this book will change your mind.

NATIVE PLANTS REFLECT A UNIQUE SENSE OF PLACE

Early explorers and settlers were awed by the variety and profusion of wildflowers throughout what would become the state of California. Hillsides in spring were painted gold, red, and yellow, and flowering shrubs added frosty blue and snowy white to the landscape. In the heat of summer, the wonderful smells of soft gray sages and sagebrush spiced the air. The landscape was humming with bees.

The beautiful colors, fresh scents, and intriguing sounds were a product of California's native plants. When we say "native plants" we mean those species that have grown in a given area since before European contact—i.e., they have evolved to live in that location specifically, and often enjoy special relationships with native fauna.

Yet as immigrants arrived in the region, homesick for eastern woods and English gardens, they created landscapes of plants that were

Fountain grass, in the foreground, a nonnative invasive plant that is commonly sold for garden use. It has spread through wildlands, endangering lovely native plants like the giant coreopsis on this slope in Santa Monica.

familiar to them. Also, developers, trying to entice newcomers, have for more than a century advertised the region as a tropical paradise, often misrepresenting the dry California that, if you look at it the right way, is its own kind of wonderland. The ready availability of water for irrigation has allowed gardeners to try their hands at growing plants from all over the world, and they have enjoyed remarkable success. (You'll hear these plants referred to as "exotic" or "nonnative.") The result of all of this is that today gardens and landscapes across the country—indeed, worldwide—exhibit the same kind of uniformity as many other man-made features, like shopping malls. Thirsty impatiens color gardens in arid lands just as they do those in the wet, semitropical climes; a mall in California looks much the same as one in Nebraska or Maine.

We have lost our sense of place. Our California gardens should be filled with plants that thrive in a land of abundant sunshine and little water. The summer dormancy of our native species should remind us of the coming winter rains that awaken them and refresh us. We should work with the land rather than against it.

NATIVE PLANTS SUPPORT BIODIVERSITY

Although renewing our sense of place is an excellent reason for gardening with native plants, environmental concerns may well provide even more persuasive motivation. The most compelling argument that I have read for planting natives is made by Douglas Tallamy in *Bringing Nature Home*. This call to action, first published in 2007 and then rereleased in 2009, is sobering. Tallamy explains that scientists believe that only 3 to 5 percent of land in the contiguous United States remains undisturbed by human activity. The country is covered with 4 million linear miles of roads, 43,480 square miles of blacktop, and

A pipevine butterfly on De La Mina lilac verbena. Butterfly larvae require host plants in the pipevine family.

Nursery workers prepare plants for sale.

62,500 square miles of sterile lawn, and this "progress" continues at an accelerating pace. The consequential loss of biological diversity is heartbreaking. But faced with all of this bad news, Tallamy offers an alternative: convert your sterile suburban gardens to rich natural habitats with local native plants.

Although nonnatives can provide food and shelter for some birds, lizards, and butterflies, most wildlife, and especially endangered wildlife, are specialists adapted to the plants and animals with which they evolved. For example, while butterflies may feed on nectar from both native and nonnative flowers, their caterpillars are frequently very picky about what they can eat, many of them preferring native species. Since nearly all of our wildlands have been impacted by development, we can no longer ignore the habitat value of our own back yards if we wish to preserve other wildlife species, as well as the general health of the planet.

NATIVE PLANTS ARE EASY TO GROW

It would be disingenuous to suggest that native plants require little or no care just because they are adapted to their locale. To the contrary, native plants have a reputation for being difficult to grow, and gardeners new to them sometimes complain about their early attempts. One issue they confront is that it can be delicate business transplanting nursery-grown native plants into a garden. The pampered young things—which, like most commercially grown plants, were probably started from cuttings—will have been regularly watered in the nursery, and until they acquire two or three years' bulk in your garden, they will need help through the hot, dry summers. However, if you water them too much or too frequently, you'll run the risk of creating fungal and bacterial conditions that can leave your native plants vulnerable to disease. Finding the right balance is key.

By contrast, common nonnative horticultural plants seem a lot easier. Although most will require copious watering throughout their lives, they have been selected and bred to withstand a wide variety of soil conditions, a feature that appeals to gardeners coast to coast. So while it's true that native plants *do* require some new knowledge, I'm here to tell you that once you understand them, natives are easy to grow.

WILD GARDENING IS RELAXING AND FUN

Each time I return to my yard after a hard day in the noise and confusion of life in urban America, my breathing slows as I hear birdsong, smell the spicy scent of wild sages, and see the colorful butterflies floating through the air. Unlike the yards of some of my neighbors

NINE REASONS TO GROW NATIVES

1. **Create good habitat.** Welcome native birds, insects, and butterflies to your yard by creating useful habitat. The best habitat is one with a variety of native plants appropriate to your locale. If you plant it, they will come. There will be no need to get in the car and drive for an hour to enjoy nature when it is right outside your door.

2. **Save water.** Many nonnative plants require supplemental water to thrive in our Mediterranean and desert climates. By planting natives, you will save water, and you can also enjoy longer periods of travel without worrying that your plants will be dead should the sprinkler system fail.

3. **Say good-bye to toxic chemicals.** Does walking through the aisle of garden chemicals at home improvement stores make your eyes itch and your nose run? Why would you want to have these toxic chemicals in your own yard? Native plants make it possible to enjoy a natural, toxin-free yard without worrying about health risks for adults, children, pets, and wildlife.

4. **Treat your senses.** Tickle your taste buds with sweet wild strawberries and piquant sage. Get a whiff of the spicy aroma of sagebrush. Stroke the smooth, sinuous bark of manzanita. Feast your eyes on the festive blues, pinks, and yellows of spring and the subtle, relaxing grays and tans of summer. Enjoy a symphony of birdsong year-round. Native plants can bring all this to you.

5. **Enhance your sense of time.** Although Californians have become accustomed to bright-green lawns and colorful flowers throughout the year, it is in observing the cycle of colors in the natural world that we can best appreciate each season and take note of time as months and years pass.

6. **Feel at home.** When returning from travels afar, the sweet, spicy, and earthy smells of a familiar environment help to settle

you firmly in your own home, giving you an unmistakable sense of place and belonging.

7. **End the tyranny of mow and blow.** All gardens need maintenance. Lawn-dominated yards, though, require an endless repetition of mowing, blowing, watering, and applying chemicals. In contrast, native plants are easy to grow and call for minimal care once you understand the remarkable adaptations they have made to live in this unique climate. In a well-planned garden, once the plants get comfortable you won't need to do as much maintenance.

8. **Feel good about being part of the solution.** The environmental forecast is not good, but it feels great to know you can do something about it. One little garden may not matter much, but you can help the movement catch on so it spreads from yard to yard. When the news gets you down, a lizard sunning herself on a rock in your garden can lift you up.

9. **Have fun in the garden.** Gardening with native plants is a great adventure. If it isn't enjoyable, you are doing something wrong. Celebrate your successes and learn from your mistakes, but never stop having fun in the garden.

California fuchsias, purple sage, and buckwheat display late-summer color in Rancho Santa Ana Botanic Garden's Cultivar Garden.

who must apply pesticides and herbicides to keep their lawns weed-free and green, there are never any small flags warning of the presence of toxic chemicals in my yard—because I never use them. My water bill is low, and it continues to decrease as I gradually replace my lawn with more-appropriate plants. It has taken some time to learn about native gardening, but the learning is fun and the reward worthwhile.

THREE APPROACHES TO GARDENING

Creating a new garden can be overwhelming. Where to start? Before getting into the details of your yard and what plants might grow well there, I want to outline three different approaches to converting your yard into a native garden. On one extreme, you can tear everything out and begin with a blank slate. On the other, you can replace plants here and there, allowing a new landscape to emerge gradually. Most people do something in between. There are advantages and disadvantages to each approach, and the best approach for you will be the one that meets your personal needs, desires, and resources, while taking into account your specific garden conditions.

THE BOLD APPROACH

What kind of gardener are you? Do you have the guts, energy, and money to erase the current reality and create a new one? If you do, you have my deep admiration. If well designed and executed, the end result can be a beautiful, coherent, and sustainable garden that will last for years.

As with any approach, however, there are pros and cons to this method. When all is said and done, replacing a conventional garden with a wild one will require fewer resources to maintain and will invite more wildlife, but getting there isn't so straightforward. Without a deep understanding of the conditions and natural history of the area, it's easy to make costly and frustrating mistakes.

Nevertheless, if you are willing to take the chance, possibly with the help of a professional who understands both you and your garden, a functioning habitat can be yours in less time than you may imagine.

Before: This garden on the side of my house consisted of a thin, weak lawn and small, feeble shrubs in April 2002.

After: Several years later, in April 2009, the lawn has disappeared and native shrubs have filled in. The organic mulch groundcover requires little care and is visually calming.

Following a year of two of "settling in," the plants in your new garden will take off. By year five it will be hard to remember how bare everything looked initially.

Pros:

- You don't have to worry about the needs of existing plants.
- It is easier to create a coherent landscape when it is designed and executed all at once.
- The whole garden makeover can be completed in a reasonable time frame.
- A fully designed garden can require few inputs and only moderate to low effort once it matures a bit.
- Your garden will quickly provide excellent habitat.

Cons:

- The cost of landscaping an entire property can be high.
- Since you will be doing everything at once, you will not have the luxury to learn as you go along, and mistakes may be big and highly visible.
- Properly done, an immature landscape looks bare and sparse, especially if all mature trees and shrubs have been removed.
- You may make your neighbors nervous.

THE GRADUAL APPROACH

Cautious gardeners who prefer to work slowly, experimenting with very small areas or even individual plants, occupy the other end of the spectrum. If you find yourself more closely aligned with them, you might wonder whether you can ever get the garden you want just by replacing single plants here and there with more desirable ones.

Alas, the answer is probably not. If the new plants you want to put in are better adapted to your climate than your existing garden plants, you will have a difficult incompatibility, kind of like a married couple in which one sleeps hot and the other cold. Their solution may be an

This small collection of potted native dudleyas demonstrates one way to begin to get to know native plants.

electric blanket with dual controls, but in the garden it can be difficult to adjust the irrigation to meet the needs of two very different plants that are sharing the same bed. If you water for the drinker, the other plant will probably drown, and furthermore, you will not be conserving water, which is one of the best reasons to grow a native garden in the first place. But keep it too dry and the old-timers will shrivel and die. The only solution may be to apply water with a hose, plant by plant according to their needs—a slow and tedious practice.

If you still want to give native plants a try but cannot bring yourself to bolder action, your best bet might be with California natives that accept and need water all year long. These plants are usually found along streams and creeks, and they often thrive in shade, since riparian and wetland areas commonly support lush arboreal growth. Finding native plants that accept full sun, summer heat, and year-round water is a challenge, but there are some. I have included a list of thirsty California native plants starting on page 184 in Appendix A.

There is also another simple way to work slowly. Look around your garden. Try to locate areas that do not receive supplemental water. These may be perfect pockets in which to tuck a few new native plants. They will need irrigation to get started, but once they settle in, you can turn off the water and see how they do.

Once you have grown a few natives and enjoyed their beauty and the thrill of watching the butterflies and birds they attract, you will certainly be ready to act more boldly.

Pros:

- Landscaping expenses are spread out over a longer period of time.

- Mistakes are so small, no one need know about them at all.

- You can learn as you go along.

- Your neighbors won't freak out, since they may not even know what you are up to.

- Since you will be working very gradually, you will never have an immature landscape that looks bare and sparse.

Cons:

- It is very difficult to change your garden practices when most of the existing plants remain in place. If it is a high-water-use garden, it will remain so.

- If you want to incorporate more sustainable plants that require less water, fertilizer, and maintenance, you will have to provide care for them individually so that the existing plants continue to receive the resources they are adapted to.

- A complete garden makeover can take a long time.

THE SOMEWHERE-IN-BETWEEN APPROACH

Most of us fall somewhere between Conan the Destroyer and Nervous Nellie, and that is fortunate, because this moderate approach has much going for it. By "moderate" I mean you are transforming your garden

This gardener carved out a small corner of her yard to plant with natives, including a native valley oak. Irrigation must be adjusted to meet the needs of both the low-water-use natives and the high-water-use lawn.

by landscaping small portions of your yard at a time, as opposed to doing all of it at once or merely changing individual plants here and there.

This approach is extremely adaptable to your needs and garden conditions. For example, you may wish to start with the back yard, where you can feel more comfortable making mistakes away from the curious eyes of your neighbors. Possibly you have large mature trees and shrubs that you want to preserve in one area, but there are other sections that can use some sprucing up. And then there are those who, like me, prefer to create new habitat gardens as a way of gradually whittling away at large expanses of lawn.

There are some words of caution, however, for those following this moderate approach. Keep in mind the cultural requirements of existing plants as you introduce new plants with different needs. This is especially important for mature trees and shrubs. Not only must you continue to provide the best horticultural conditions for these plants, you should also take care to disturb their roots as little as possible when gardening nearby.

As you change small areas of your yard, try to work toward a unified, holistic garden plan. Make connections between sections. Look beyond the new garden spaces to see how existing plants and structures provide a backdrop. Consider how these new gardens will look in relation to the rest of the yard when the plants mature.

Finally, in the spirit of keeping gardening fun, the section-by-section approach allows you to control the amount of work, money, and time you invest. Never let it overwhelm you and sap the enjoyment out of something that should be pleasurable. If you keep things under control and focus on what you have accomplished, gardening can be a fulfilling lifelong hobby rather than a never-ending, burdensome chore.

Pros:

• You can experiment without risking the loss of your entire landscape.

• Although you are limited by existing conditions and the needs of trees and other plants in nearby spaces, you can modify your garden incrementally, learning by trial and error as you go.

• As you gradually build knowledge about which plants do well in your garden and which plants you like best, you can use that information when you expand into other portions of your yard.

Cons:

• Unless you are careful, your yard can look like a hodgepodge of unrelated garden beds.

• It can take a long time for your entire yard to have a completed look.

• You are constrained by the needs of existing plants.

Once you have decided which approach you are most comfortable with, it is time to make plans. First, let's get to know your yard.

WHEN TO PLANT

Although it is possible to plant throughout the year in much of California, you will have greater success if you wait until late fall or winter

A summer garden in the San Fernando Valley gets a small bit of water to keep it hydrated. Most of the native plants are dormant through the long, hot dry season, making this time less than optimal for planting.

to put the plants in the ground. Air and soil temperatures are cooler, and usually winter rains provide needed moisture. Although most new plantings will require supplemental water regardless of when they are planted, these tender young plants will have a better chance of becoming established when they can benefit from rain and/or irrigation water delivered during the natural rainy season.

Nevertheless, the debate over an "ideal" planting season is loud and cantankerous. Much of it comes down to the differences in garden location, which can determine whether off-season planting is successful or not. For example, while inland areas are often hot and dry during the spring and summer, some coastal areas have moderate temperatures all year, making spring and summer planting more tenable there. Also important is the type of plants and their particular

Students planting in a city park in South Pasadena on a cloudy day in January.

needs. Native plants that naturally grow along rivers or in marshes require water throughout the year. Since they are adapted to continuously wet conditions, they usually do fine planted during summer as long as they receive adequate water. And although desert plants need very little water overall, they do experience occasional monsoonal rainstorms in summer, so planting and watering them during the dry season is not out of the question. Plants adapted to year-round water or summer monsoonal rains are, of course, better able to accept dry-season irrigation than those that naturally go dormant during the summer drought (think chaparral or coastal sage scrub plants), but again, every garden is different, so check your conditions and then schedule your planting accordingly. If you do attempt off-season planting, first check out the tips in the section "Keep Your Garden Alive," starting on page 157.

GARDEN INTERLUDE: SIDEWALK WILDERNESS

My eyes scan the emerald-green yard when we take possession of our ninety-year-old Craftsman house. Both the structure and yard are daunting; I never pictured myself living in a historic house of this size, not to mention one set on a third of an acre of suburban land. There are five mature trees casting welcome shade in the front and back yards, and the rest is grass, with small foundation beds around the house. Colorful but thirsty impatiens make this look like the home of June and Ward from *Leave It to Beaver*. Lavish amounts of water are needed to keep it all looking bright, and to keep it neat requires an ongoing regimen of mowing, edging, raking, and sweeping—not to mention the recommended fertilizers and weed killers.

Since we first arrived in Southern California in 1996, I knew I wanted a wild garden, and here was my chance to build one. My taste veers toward the wild side—my desk, my clothing, my purse, my mind, all exhibit untidiness, with interesting objects scattered about—and I was excited to create the garden to match. Looking at my desk right now I see pencils and paperclips in an array of colors, a snapshot of my family all smiling into a camera we'd set on a timer to capture the moment, a plastic paperweight with glitter floating around a picture of my daughter and our dog, and many

My house in 1999.

other random objects filling the space. It's cluttered even in what I'd consider this current state of extreme neatness. For me, a comfortable garden needs a similar mix of order and interest. Unusual plants, textured rocks, sculptural pieces of dead wood—all have places in my garden because they are objects that capture my attention and imagination.

But I digress. Back at the house in the late 1990s, the front yard is shaded by two large trees—an avocado and a deodar cedar—and I am amazed that the previous owners were somehow able to keep the lawn beneath them green. I doubted I would be so skilled, but I also knew this location was no place to start a new garden. I wasn't about to make drastic changes near unfamiliar specimen trees, and at the very least I knew that an abrupt transformation to the ground near them might be harmful. I figured it was best to make as few changes as possible at first.

The back yard also has mature trees, including a large coast live oak and two large fruit-bearing avocados. Not only is there a limited amount of sun for a garden, but again I knew it was safest not to mess with the mature trees until I had lived with them for a while.

The house is on a corner lot. On the east side, against the street, is a long strip of ground, 6 feet wide and 170 feet long. From the magnolia near the southern end of the strip it is pretty much a straight shot for about 160 feet. The sprinklers there are only partially functional, and water sprays everywhere; some hits the grass, but much of it lands on the street and the sidewalk. Mowing is easily completed in four long laps, but edging is interminable, as the electric weed-whip that was intended to make short work of this job gets tangled frequently. The bed gets quite a bit of sun, shaded only by the magnolia at the south end, and I can see that whatever I plant will not have to compete with established trees for sunlight, water, or nutrients. It is perfect. The parkway will be my first wild garden.

So the project begins with the long strip between the street and sidewalk: a curb garden. I pick up a shovel and start digging out the grass. Just as I finish removing a small rectangle of weedy lawn, my neighbor stops by to mention that there is a city ordinance that regulates parkway landscaping. I thank him for the information and think nothing more of it.

GET TO KNOW YOUR YARD

GETTING TO KNOW your yard is like getting to know another person. It takes years, and even when you think you know everything there is to know, you can still be surprised. Nevertheless, as with personal relationships, we need to take a leap of faith if we want that connection to grow, and part of moving ahead is accepting that we will make mistakes.

Some gardeners pride themselves for being able to grow plants that have needs that are not easily met in their own gardens. These "experts" may take on the challenge of growing notoriously finicky varieties in adverse conditions, like trying to cultivate a tropical orchid, susceptible to a myriad of diseases, in a hot climate with little rain and extremely low humidity. That's fine for some people, but not me! I admire the gardener who can create a beautiful, peaceful landscape doing as little work as he or she wants. To accomplish this feat, a masterful gardener knows her garden and selects plants that are well adapted to its conditions. A friend of mine describes his gardening technique as "tough love." He selects plants that he believes will make it in his garden and then he just lets them go: no pampering, no babying. If they die, they did not belong there. Now, this may not be the best design strategy, but over time only those plants well adapted to his yard remain, and so he proves his point. If he is happy with the way the garden looks and the amount of time it demands, then he is by my standards a masterful gardener. The first step to any garden project, therefore, is getting to know your yard, including its climate, sun, soil, and water profiles.

CLIMATE

Coastal California's climate is for the most part arid, with annual rainfall usually below twenty inches, nearly all of which comes during the

Water cascades down the San Gabriel River following heavy rains in the winter of 2005.

cooler winter months. Temperatures are moderate. Those who have lived here for many years are accustomed to this weather pattern, but to outsiders it is very unusual. In fact, this climate occurs in only five distinct regions of the world, covering in total only about 2 percent of Earth's landmass. The largest of the five regions is around the Mediterranean Basin in Europe, hence use of the term "Mediterranean" to describe this climate wherever it occurs. A Mediterranean climate can be described quite simply as hot, dry summers and cool, wet winters. In addition to the Mediterranean Basin and California, this unusual climate can be found in southwestern and southern Australia, central Chile, and South Africa's Western Cape province.

Southern California can be very hot and dry, and many are tempted to classify our region as desert. Palm Springs, Indio, and Barstow are indeed typified by their desert climate, but coastal areas and inland valleys with annual rainfall ranging from seven inches in Riverside to fifteen in Los Angeles, though still considered arid or semiarid, are not deserts.

In these regions, rain, when it comes at all, falls during four to six months of the year. The rainy season begins in November or December

Afternoon rainstorms in September are more common in Spain than in our hotter, drier Mediterranean climate.

and tapers off in March and April. Accumulations vary from a few inches in some years to thirty or more in others. Winter rainstorms can be very heavy, bringing several inches in a twenty-four-hour period.

Wherever you live, this rule holds true: your garden will be most successful if you choose plants that are well adapted to your climate.

SUN

Many nurseries and growers provide information on how much sun a plant prefers. Plants that thrive in full sun often sport tags with a small yellow sun icon. Those that need or accept a bit of shade will be marked with a half-darkened circle, and plants best grown in full shade may have a dark circle with no cheerful rays. If only the reality were so simple!

Consider these fairly common situations: Imagine a garden bed located north of a two-story house. It gets full sun in summer, but in winter the sun does not rise above the peak of the roof, leaving the garden in full shade for several months of the year. In another garden, a deciduous tree may cast shade during the summer, but its bare

A child plants a monkeyflower in a park on a warm January morning.

branches leave the garden in full sun throughout the winter. The sun/shade designation for these gardens changes seasonally and isn't easily defined by a nursery tag.

To further complicate this very simple notion, a given plant may need a different exposure in slightly different climates. For example, some California native plants thrive in full sun along the coast, where the temperature is moderate and fog is common, while inland they do best with afternoon shade, especially in the summer. In this case the cryptic plant instructions may be "full sun to part shade," meaning, at least in this case, full sun in coastal areas, part shade inland. However, "full sun to part shade" can also mean that the plant has a range of sun tolerance in any location, from full sun in hot, dry climates to partial shade in cooler, wetter areas.

Not only does location influence exposure requirements, the time of day that your plant receives its sun can also affect how well it grows. Afternoon shade is very different from morning shade in some areas. The former is somewhat easier on plants in hot climates, for instance, since they are shaded during the hottest time of day. Furthermore, morning sun dries up nighttime moisture on leaves and soil, meaning plants that don't get sun until the afternoon are at greater risk for problems with moisture-loving snails, slugs, mildew, and fungal leaf spot disease. If, though, you are trying to grow desert plants that thrive in heat and light, afternoon sun may be just the ticket.

I despair at what this short but complicated description of exposure will do to my readers. Hopefully you will not turn away in disgust before I can assure you that what looks like chaos is actually not so bad if you follow a handful of useful guidelines.

For starters, when working with native plants, we can go beyond the limited wisdom of the nursery tag and look to see where they naturally occur. If you plan to grow a plant you often see thriving in the wild in full sun, by all means place it in the sunniest spot you can find in your garden. Keep your eyes open to see whether this same plant is sometimes found growing in a bit of shade, though, and also observe the plant in cultivated environments such as botanical and personal gardens. Under what conditions does it seem to be happiest?

Armed with these observations, take your best shot, placing your plants where you think they will flourish. If a particular specimen always seems to be hot and dried out after it has been in the ground for several months, you may want to try to move it to—or plant another one in—a less sunny location to see if it fares better with different exposure conditions. Gardening is a bit science and a bit art. As you learn and grow with your garden, you'll figure out what works for you and build your confidence, and more of your plants will thrive.

SOIL

Not only is gardening full of caveats and maybes, it is also a contact sport. You must get dirty to be good at it. That means, literally, getting in touch with the soil.

Soil is a highly complex, dynamic system. It consists of particulate matter (both organic and inorganic), water, air, and a myriad of biological organisms. Soil also changes with depth. The topsoil—generally the first two to eight inches from the surface—is full of micro- and macro-organisms and is where most of the biological activities occur. Roots acquire nearly all of their water, air, and nutrients from the topsoil. The subsoil and bedrock below the topsoil contain less water and air, and have little biological activity, although roots and other living organisms can move minerals and elements from these underlying layers into the plants and ultimately into the topsoil, through the decomposition of fallen leaves and branches.

Understanding soil is an essential element in selecting plants that will be most likely to succeed with the least modification to your existing conditions. There are, however, cases when the soil has been so altered that little or nothing can grow in it, so if even weeds are absent from your soil, you should consider professional soil testing to figure out what your problem is and how you can fix it. Three common causes of unproductive soil are: (1) a buildup of salts in poorly drained soils from years of excessive fertilizing, (2) compaction of heavy clay soil from construction activity, and (3) the removal of topsoil during construction. Each of these problems will require significant remediation with professional help.

The good news, however, is that most of us do not have these issues. So what does the home gardener need to know about soil to be successful? The five elements to consider are texture, organics, microorganisms, structure, and chemistry. Let's take a look at what each one means for your garden.

An exuberant Riverside garden in heavy clay soil.

TEXTURE

Soil texture is determined by mineral content. It describes the prevalence of large, medium, and small mineral particulates. Generally speaking, soils composed of mostly large particulates are sandy, soils with mostly medium-sized particulates are silty, and soils whose composition is more than 30 percent very small particulates are clayey.

Sandy soil is lean, fast draining, and difficult to compact. Clay soil is slow draining, rich in plant nutrients, and easily compacted. Silty soil is somewhere in between. Loamy soil has a good mix of all three—40 percent sand, 40 percent silt, and 20 percent clay—and is considered by most gardeners to be ideal, especially if it includes organic matter as well. But although this predominating wisdom may be true for common commercially produced plants, native plants come from a wider range of locales and therefore have different needs. Of the California natives, many desert and coastal sage scrub plants do best in lean, sandy soils with excellent drainage, and many woodland

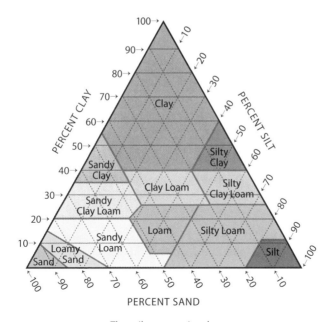

The soil-texture triangle.

plants may require greater amounts of clay to hold nutrients and water. There is no one-size-fits-all soil when it comes to native gardening.

ORGANICS

Healthy soil contains organic matter, like bits of wood, seeds, leaves, worm "castings" (that's poop, not to put too fine a point on it), and so on. Living organisms create these materials, which not only provide nutrients for plants (and animals) but also change the physical structure and chemical makeup of the soil in which they grow.

Desert and scrub plants grow in lean soils with limited organic matter, whereas woodland plants are adapted to the conditions of organic-rich soils—that is, soils with higher concentrations of nutrients—which tend to retain moisture and heat.

MICROORGANISMS

Microorganisms have a profound and complex effect on soil chemistry, structure, and biology, and we are only now beginning to understand their significance in soil and the role they play in plant health and disease. Just as we are coming to appreciate the importance of "good bacteria" for human digestion and health, we are learning that the correct types and balance of fungi and bacteria are critical to healthy soil.

This knowledge has led to the proliferation of soil amendments containing microorganisms said to improve soil quality through a system of mutually beneficial interactions between fungi and plants. Scientists are currently studying these symbiotic relationships, called *mycorrhizae,* in hopes of developing commercial products that could further improve growing conditions, especially where soil integrity is compromised. Unfortunately, there is little scientific support that the addition of commercially produced mycorrhizal amendments will improve growing conditions, and until there is solid evidence supporting their use in gardening—that is, data beyond the anecdotal claims of people who stand to gain from the sale of related products—it is reasonable to work with the soil you have, allowing natural processes to gradually improve growing conditions.

STRUCTURE

While texture tells you something about the mineral composition of soil, the structure of soil depends on the interplay of both mineral and organic materials and living matter (i.e., the network of fungi, bacteria, and macro-organisms like worms and roots). The term "structure" refers to the arrangement of soil particles into clumps, or "peds" in the scientific lexicon. Air, water, and nutrients move through cracks between peds.

Over time, plants and animals improve soil structure. Worms not only help decompose vegetative matter and leave behind worm castings, they also create pores in the soil as they move through it. Gophers, so disliked by gardeners for chomping down on newly planted specimens, can actually be helpful if they excavate pockets in heavy clay soils that would otherwise be impenetrable. As plants grow and eventually die, their roots create cracks and holes in soil as well. Soil structure is delicate. Rototilling, hoeing, and driving heavy equipment on soil—especially heavy, wet soil—can damage the structure, which takes a long time to recover. Treat your soil gently and your plants will thank you for it.

CHEMISTRY

Now that we've seen how soils can vary physically in texture and structure, let's look at how they can vary chemically. Fertility, pH, salinity, and toxicity are four basic chemical properties that affect garden soils. Native plants are adapted to the natural chemical properties of local soils, and so, generally speaking, adding fertilizer or otherwise amending soil is not only unnecessary but it can create adverse growing conditions. Unless you are experiencing more serious problems, you shouldn't need to have your soil tested. If you suspect your soil is suffering from a chemical issue, however, the following discussion will help you determine whether you need a more in-depth analysis.

Fertility Nitrogen, phosphorus, and potassium are three essential elements that are often supplemented through commercial fertilizers. The relative amounts of these three elements is listed on bags of fertilizer as the percentage ratio of nitrogen to phosphorus to potassium, or NPK. A ratio of 10:5:5, for example, means that a ten-pound bag has one pound of nitrogen (10 percent), and one half-pound each of phosphoric acid and pot ash. California soils tend to be relatively low in nitrogen and high in potassium. Since California native plants are adapted to that makeup, soil fertility should not be an issue unless the soil has been adversely altered in some way, as with some fertilizers. In fact, adding fertilizers, especially those high in nitrogen, can promote excessive plant growth that is difficult to sustain in our hot, dry climate.

In some cases, however, such as very well-drained, lean soils, the available nitrogen may be so low it could use a boost. Although it is best to select plants adapted to this specific condition, supplementing soil with a modest amount of fertilizer can help new plants become established. Be sparing with fertilizer, using it at one-quarter to one-half of the recommended amount. Adding organic mulch will also increase soil fertility over time, reducing the need to use fertilizer in the future.

A final note on soil fertility: Topsoil develops slowly—so slowly it is often considered a nonrenewable resource—so if yours is compromised you might need to have it replaced. Topsoil is sometimes scraped from a construction site before new homes are built, and the subsoil left behind usually exhibits low fertility. If topsoil replacement is required, you'll want to make sure it is: (1) collected ethically, without creating environmental harm to another site, (2) disease-free, and (3) taken from a local source with similar growing conditions.

pH   Soils vary in pH values from acidic (below 7) to basic (above 7), although most are very nearly neutral (with a value of exactly 7, like water). Acidic soils occur in wetter regions, especially in soils with good drainage and high levels of organic matter. Certain plants, such as azaleas, rhododendrons, and blueberries, are adapted to acidic soils and do not do well in basic, or alkaline, soil. Much of California, however, has alkaline soil, and plants that naturally grow in these areas (particularly the hot and dry portions of the state) are adapted to higher pH values. Changing your soil's pH can be difficult, and as with other soil modifications, it is better to grow natives that are a good fit for your soil's natural pH.

Salinity Salt buildup is another serious problem that can affect soil chemistry. Rapid evaporation of water from the surface of poorly drained soils—especially if the water was high in salts, as is the case with some irrigation and seawater—can cause high salinity, as can excessive use of fertilizers. It is difficult to remediate saline soils yourself, so seek professional assistance if a soil test reveals that you have this problem. Remediation may include leaching out the salts by watering heavily with fresh water, amending the soil with gypsum (calcium sulfate) to replace sodium ions with calcium, or planting salt-excreting plants and then removing them after they have grown for a while.

Toxicity Heavy metals or other toxins can accumulate in urban or industrial areas, so it is important to know the history of the land prior to residential development. Common contributors to soil toxicity include lead-based paints used before the 1970s and pressure-treated wood—often used for decks and other outdoor structures—which may leave behind chromium and arsenic. Test the soil if you suspect or are concerned about the presence of toxins, especially if you are planning to grow edibles, as lead and other heavy metals can be ingested from hand-to-mouth contact with contaminated soil. (Few toxins are incorporated into the living tissue of the plants, although some plants do take up more heavy metals than others.) Washing all garden-grown foods, wearing gloves, and washing your hands after working in the garden will limit your exposure to toxins. Children especially should not ingest toxins, so if you have kids, it is advisable to get your soil tested.

THREE EASY SOIL TESTS

One of the most important things to know about garden soil is how quickly water drains through it. The following DIY tests will help you determine where your soil falls on the spectrum of excellent to poor drainage.

Simple soil test: Dig a hole, fill it with water, and let it drain. Then set up rulers, refill the hole with water, and measure how far it goes down in fifteen minutes. If the water level drops an inch or more in fifteen minutes, you have well-drained soil. If you cannot detect a drop in water level in an hour, you have poorly drained soil. Measurements between these extremes indicate moderate drainage. These are only general guidelines to help you select plants most likely to succeed.

Percolation test Dig a hole approximately ten inches deep and eight inches wide. Fill it with water and then let it drain. Now refill it, but this time record how long it takes for the hole to empty. Alternatively, you can measure the water level in the hole after the second filling and take repeat measurements in fifteen-minute intervals.

Since soil texture and drainage can vary within a garden, dig holes in several locations for a more accurate reading of your overall drainage profile. The soil in my garden drains quickly—approximately two inches every fifteen minutes. Although there are various definitions of fast, medium, and slow, most gardeners agree that in soil with medium drainage the water level declines roughly one to three inches per hour. Sandy soils may drain within seconds, the water disappearing as you watch, and in soils with a lot of clay it can sometimes take hours, or even days, for the water to subside.

When you roll it in your hands, clay soil sticks together whereas loamy or sandy soil crumbles and breaks apart.

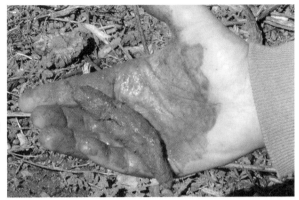

Mud snake test Thoroughly wet some soil taken from a few inches below the surface. Roll it into a "snake" about one inch thick and a few inches long. If the soil falls apart and refuses to form a thick, meaty snake, it is probably sandy. Soil high in clay holds together well and feels slippery. Again, these are the extremes, and most soil falls somewhere in between. Soils high in clay often have poor drainage.

Mayonnaise jar test Dig out approximately one cup of soil from a couple of inches below the surface or mulch layer. Place it in a clear quart-sized jar, like one used for mayonnaise. Add water, and then skim off the organic material that floats to the top. Now cover the jar and

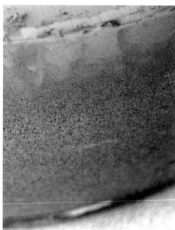

The jar on the left has soil with larger particulates and less clay than the jar on the right. The garden with more clay has poor drainage.

shake it. Watch as the heavy sand particles quickly fall to the bottom. It will take many hours for the clay particles to sort themselves out, so leave the jar undisturbed overnight. The next day, you should be able to see three distinct layers: sand, silt, and clay.

The commercial horticultural community has decided the "ideal" soil is composed of 10 to 20 percent clay and roughly equal amounts of silt and sand. Soil, however, is neither good nor bad (unless it has been so altered that nothing at all will grow in it), and so again, the best way to create a healthy and successful garden is to work with what you have. If your soil test shows more than 20 percent clay, you probably do not have excellent, or even good, drainage. More than 50 percent sand in the jar indicates a well-drained soil, which usually is lower in nutrients. Whatever your soil type, select plants that are likely to thrive in those conditions, since modifying soil can be both difficult and expensive. Remember also that gardens do change over time, and that includes their soils. Heavy, compacted clay soil will develop improved structure and drainage as new plants take hold, extending their roots through the soil, while worms and other insects create pores and incorporate organics. Many of our native plants do better in lean soils, but I also have some tips for gardening with more difficult soils.

GROWING NATIVES IN CLAY SOIL

What is clay soil?

- Very small particle sizes
- Lots of tiny pores
- Generally good fertility
- Undisturbed clay soil can have good structure (aggregates and holes), providing plants with accessible nutrients, water, and air.

How do I know if I have clay soil?

- Water runs off rather than penetrating.
- It is hard to dig when dry (non-friable).
- It takes a long time for it to dry out after a long, soaking rain.
- It may crack due to expansion when wet and contraction when dry.
- The soil percolation test indicates poor drainage.
- If lightly squeezed, it resists breaking and will stretch into a long, thin ribbon.
- It feels slippery.

How amending clay soil goes wrong:

- If you add less than 50 percent by volume of coarse sand, you are likely to create concrete. Fine sand makes the problem even worse.
- "Soil conditioners" such as lime and gypsum change the soil chemistry and should only be used if a soil test indicates specific deficiencies. These products can lead to an excess of calcium and magnesium in the soil, and lime can increase soil pH. Western soils—often naturally alkaline (i.e., with high pH values)—may be damaged by increased alkalinity.
- Drainage and barrier problems can develop between native and amended soils.

- Rototilling clay soil destroys whatever structure the soil has, and over time it usually causes more problems than it solves.

What to do:

- If there is little growing in the soil, do a soil test to determine and correct the specific problems.

- Select plants appropriate to the type of soil you have, which in this case means avoiding plants that require good or excellent drainage. (For a list of native plants that thrive in clay soil, see page 189 of Appendix A.) To increase variety in your garden, grow some plants in containers or raised beds (at least two feet deep, and prepared so water does not accumulate at the interface where the two soils meet); here you can easily modify soil conditions to meet the needs of your chosen plants.

- Only garden when the soil is slightly moist. Working dry or saturated clay soil destroys its structure, which can take a long time to recover. Do not walk or drive vehicles on wet clay soil.

- Apply a two- to four-inch layer of mulch to protect soil from compaction, increase water penetration, reduce runoff, and improve structure over time.

- When planting, dig holes wider but not deeper than the root ball, and roughen the sides of the planting hole with a garden cultivator. Backfill with native soil, and do not add amendments to the planting hole. If you feel that you must add amendments, gradually diminish the amount as you work away from the plant to the surrounding soil.

- Apply water slowly to allow it to penetrate with no runoff; some sprinkler controllers have on/off cycling to allow time for deeper water infiltration. Check for moisture several inches below the surface, and do not water again until the soil is moderately dry.

- Grow durable wildflowers such as California poppies to begin the process of developing good soil structure. A layer of coarse gravel mulch may help the seedlings germinate and penetrate the soil.

- Be patient. As plants start to grow in clay soil, root growth and other biological activity will gradually improve its structure. Soil structure will continue to improve over time as long as there is minimal disturbance of the soil.

GROWING NATIVES IN SANDY SOIL

What is sandy soil?

- Relatively large particle sizes
- Nutrients wash out, resulting in lean soil

How do I know if I have sandy soil?

- Water soaks in and drains through rapidly, allowing it to dry out quickly.
- It is not easily compacted.
- The soil percolation test indicates fast drainage.

How amending sandy soil goes wrong:

- Organics and other amendments decompose or wash through sandy soil rapidly, requiring frequent replacement.
- Amendments that wash into underground water can be carried to streams, lakes, and ultimately oceans, introducing excess nutrients that can lead to harmful algal blooms.

What to do:

- If there is little growing in the soil, do a soil test to determine and correct the specific problems.
- Select plants appropriate to the type of soil you have, which in this case means avoiding varieties that require soil high in organic content. (For a list of native plants that thrive in sandy soil, see page 188 of Appendix A.) To increase variety in your

garden, grow some plants in containers or raised beds (at least two feet deep, and prepared so water does not accumulate at the interface); here you can easily modify soil conditions to meet the needs of your chosen plants.

In some cases lightly amending the soil in and around the planting hole with organic matter can help a new plant get started. Gradually decrease the amount of amendment as you work out into the surrounding soil.

- Use mulch. Organic mulch will help moderate soil temperature and reduce water loss through evaporation. It will have to be replaced frequently, but over time it, along with plants and animals, will improve the fertility of and increase the amount of organic material in your soil. Inorganic mulch is best for plants that prefer lean soil, but keep in mind that it does little to moderate soil temperature.

- Use boulders or hardscape elements like pergolas and walls to shade and protect plants. Grow sunflowers, other annual wildflowers, or short-lived perennials near new plantings to temporarily moderate heat and light.

- Be patient. As plants start to grow in sandy soil, root growth and other biological activity will gradually increase the organic content. Soil structure will slowly improve as long as there is minimal disturbance of the soil.

GROWING NATIVES IN SILTY SOIL

What is silty soil?

- Intermediate particle sizes (much larger than clay particles, yet smaller than sand)

- Soil with this texture both holds nutrients (unlike sandy soil) and yet has fairly good drainage (unlike soil high in clay).

How do I know if I have silty soil?

- Water soaks in and drains through in one to several hours, neither fast nor slow.

How amending silty soil goes wrong:

- There is usually no need to amend silty soil, especially if it is loamy silt—that is, it contains a small bit of clay and some sand along with medium-sized silt particles.

What to do:

- If there is little growing in the soil, do a soil test to determine and correct the specific problems.

- Many plants will do well in silty soil, including most of those recommended for clay and sandy soil types. If your soil drainage is on the slower side, avoid plants requiring excellent drainage.

WATER

Living in Southern California, it's all about water. The sun shines brightly almost every day of the year. Temperatures are, for the most part, moderate, and due to low humidity, even the hottest days are followed by delightfully cool nights. Precipitation rarely interferes with our fun, as those who watch the New Year's Rose Parade know. In this glorious climate, it is said we can grow just about anything. This is nearly true, so long as we do not forget the addendum: just add water.

Whether you intend to garden with supplemental irrigation or rely mostly on naturally occurring water, success will elude you unless you understand water in your garden. As noted above, water in our Mediterranean climate comes primarily during winter months in the form of rain, and that's not always reliable. Annual fluctuations in rainfall are large, and successive years of drought are common.

Though rain is scarce, water comes in the form of fog in the foothills and coastal areas.

Luckily, water can be delivered to the garden in other forms. Fog, lifting off the ocean and blowing inland, bathes some gardens in moisture through much of the year. Some of these foggy gardens dry out by afternoon, while others barely see a ray of sunshine through the mist. High-elevation gardens, in foothill or mountains areas, may receive moisture in the form of snow or runoff from nearby snowbanks, while

Rainwater from streets and sidewalks is directed into parkway gardens, conserving water and reducing urban runoff.

inland gardens may receive occasional summer thunderstorms due to monsoonal conditions.

Water also flows underground. Although the water table has fallen due to years of pumping, the channelization of streams, and reduced infiltration (meaning less water soaking into the soil due to an increase in nonpermeable surfaces like roads and buildings), water still travels below the surface naturally. Water rich in nitrogen also sometimes leaks into gardens from old sewer pipes, many of them damaged by the roots of trees. Low spots can act as sinks that collect subsurface water and cause other problems for the home gardener.

Runoff from a neighbor's irrigation or from impermeable surfaces including roofs, paths, driveways, and roads can be other sources of unexpected water in your garden. Although you may not have control over the amount of water delivered in these ways, failure to account for

This beautiful old coast live oak, which was growing in a local park, fell over suddenly one spring day. Years of excessive irrigation, due to maintenance that favored the surrounding lawn, weakened the tree's root system.

it can result in plant damage or mortality. Gardens that intentionally make use of water from these sources are referred to as "rain gardens." Rainwater harvesting is not only convenient, it is an important sustainable gardening practice, as it conserves water, reduces urban runoff, and increases rainwater soil infiltration. Again, when planning a garden, consider these and all other sources of water.

Once you have a good sense of how much water is available, where it is coming from, and how it is delivered to different parts of your yard, you need to think about how it interacts with other physical characteristics of the garden. For example, as we discussed earlier, gardens with lean, well-drained soil do not retain water well, as compared with gardens containing loamy or clay soil. Low-lying areas with heavy soil may stay wet for months without any supplemental irrigation or rainfall. Mulch also influences water retention in soil, as do wind and sun exposure.

Into this amazing and complicated system we attempt to predict which plants will do best. But don't let that intimidate you; gardens offer wonderful surprises *because* they are complex. When I first saw a willow tree standing high and dry on a mound in our local nature park, I thought someone had selected exactly the wrong plant for that location. Later I learned, to my surprise, it just had shown up on its own and, to the contrary, was exactly the right plant for that location.

This willow tree appeared in a park of its own accord in what appears to be a poorly chosen location, on a mound away from any apparent water sources. Its success indicates the presence of underground water.

Water information on plant labels, similar to sun exposure information, can be vague and simplistic and require additional interpretation and expertise. The extremes—like "Dry: no supplemental water" or "Wet: keep evenly moist"—are fairly clear, but terms like "regular" and "ample" seem relative at best. These labels also usually ignore seasonal variations in water needs. Many native plants are adapted to summer drought and wet winters, so an experienced native plant gardener will know to water natives during those winters that receive little rain, while keeping summers relatively dry to avoid root rot. In fact, overwatering, especially in summer, is probably the biggest cause of failure in native plant gardens.

In addition, water guidelines are usually meant for established plants, so the rules need to be modified for those just starting out. Young plants that have recently been transplanted have different needs than plants that have been in the garden for a couple of years. New plants often require additional water until they have bulked up and their roots have extended into the surrounding soil. This can take one to three years depending on the plant type. (Plant care during establishment is discussed in more detail in the "Keep Your Garden Alive" section, starting on page 157).

Nonetheless, water guidelines do have value. At the very least, they should be used to group plants with similar water needs. This practice, called *hydrozoning*, makes the garden easier to manage and much more likely to succeed.

Beyond that, you will need to experiment to determine what watering schedule works best for your plants. This requires observation and experience. Whenever I travel and leave my husband in charge of the yard, he requests a list with clear and precise instructions on when to water each plant. The best I can do is to tell him to "water them when needed." He does not find this amusing or helpful, and he lets me know. He is not on intimate terms with each plant, as I am, and so these vague instructions are useless. I try to provide better information, but a serious gardener should indeed follow the most obvious guideline: water as necessary.

OTHER CONDITIONS

In addition to climate, sun, soil, and water, there are several other conditions that affect how plants fare in gardens. High winds, for example, can damage brittle trees, such as palo verde, so gardens exposed to this element should be planted with hardier stock. If staked properly, a fast-growing brittle tree may survive to maturity only to break later in a major windstorm, so it's best to build your garden accordingly.

Another condition beginning gardeners often overlook is reflected heat from light-colored, west-facing walls. Although the exposure, water, and soil conditions may be appropriate for a given plant in such a location, it can fail if it's unable to withstand the high afternoon temperatures it will experience in that position. Spend time in all of the nooks and crannies of your yard to experience the many microclimates to which plants must adapt.

And finally, new plants must be compatible with existing plants and able to establish themselves among their roots, in their shade, and amid their debris. It is usually difficult for plants to establish beneath mature trees because they must compete with a large, vigorous network of roots. There are five large trees on my one-third-acre lot, so I must keep in mind that anything I plant will have to compete with these behemoth organisms. Most of the plants I add to my garden grow quite slowly, probably because they must compete with older plants for water and nutrients.

It is, however, possible to grow plants near mature trees, although it's generally best to do so beyond the tree's canopy. If the specimen tree is of great value—and most are—give it plenty of room; avoid disturbing its roots, even at the surface; and provide water and other care in accordance with its needs. When planting or putting in hardscape near mature trees, you should weigh carefully the value of the tree versus the aesthetic qualities gained by the new landscaping. With a little thought and planning, you can add plants that will look good and thrive in your garden.

GARDEN INTERLUDE:
A WET DESERT

We left the great East Coast metropolis in early summer, flying three thousand miles to our new home in the West. Arriving before our possessions, my husband, kids, and I took a mini-vacation in a fancy hotel in Pasadena. The first thing that struck all of us was the heat. And not only was it hot, it was dry. Really dry. It felt like we could not drink enough water to stay hydrated. We were pleasantly surprised each afternoon when the temperature dropped to a comfortable number in the mid-70s, but the sun was still brilliant and unrelenting. How could anything live in this desert?

A desert landscape with sparse plant coverage due to the dearth of water.

The plant community "coastal sage scrub" includes low-growing, drought-tolerant, often aromatic shrubs. Also called soft chaparral, these plants grow in higher densities than similar plants in drier desert areas.

It was sunny and hot throughout our first summer in Southern California. Every day was nearly the same. The five-day forecast almost always consisted of five identical yellow circles, a weather pattern I found strange and disorienting. I wanted to love my new home, but I longed for an afternoon thunderstorm.

If summer in its monotony was not strange enough, winter was completely bizarre. In late November, much to our relief, it finally rained. Then it rained some more. In fact, it rained for days at a time, and not just a steady, even rainfall but a full-on downpour. For the first time in my life I heard the term "El Niño," the name for the phenomenon that dumps heavy rain along the Pacific coast. Through the end of the year and the beginning of the next, the rain continued. Yes, there were periods of magnificent sunshine, often accompanied by warmth only felt in the summer back East, but then another storm would roll in from the Pacific and we'd be shivering in our rainboots. "Another Pineapple Express," the weather forecaster said. That year our rainfall totaled a respectable thirty-two inches, and it all came between the months of November and March.

The El Niño winter of 1997 taught me that we do not live in a desert. Deserts do not get that much rain! I braced myself for a return of the rains the following year, but when November came, there were only a few rainy days, nothing like the previous year. A dry December followed. Occasionally the local mountains, first shrouded in dark-gray clouds, would sparkle the next day with a brilliant white coating of snow, but my anticipation of rain turned out to be wrong. The weather forecasters rarely mentioned the Pineapple Express or El Niño, and instead they were calling it a La Niña year. For newcomers like us, it was an education. One year was as wet as my East Coast home, and the next year was so dry that we might as well have lived in the Sahara.

I learned that the pattern of cool, wet winters and hot, dry summers, along with large annual variations in rainfall, are characteristic of our Mediterranean climate. These strange surroundings left me feeling unsettled, adrift. It was my hope that gardening would help me understand my new home, just as understanding my new home would help me become a better gardener.

FORMULATE YOUR PLAN

AFTER GETTING TO know your yard, the next step in creating a wild garden is getting to know yourself. If you have already thought about your desired overall gardening approach—bold, bit-by-bit, or somewhere in between—then you have started this process. Now you need to think about how you want to use your yard; how others living with you, including pets, will influence the outdoor space; and who will be doing the gardening, both while it is being created and afterward, when it needs ongoing care.

Google Earth images of my house help me step back for a more holistic view.

A garden plan helps you identify and address your needs while taking into account your specific garden conditions. It also allows you to see the individual pieces of the project come together as a coordinated whole. We begin with a rough sketch identifying different areas and their needs, and then proceed to a more detailed, scaled plan with paths, structures, irrigation systems, and plant types. Actual plant selection is covered in a later chapter. (Specific plants are discussed in "Learn About Native Plants," starting on page 67, and plant lists for specific garden conditions can be found in the appendices, starting on page 183.)

Landscape design is a complex process, and the following section will present a broad overview to help you get started. If you are uncomfortable taking on the planning yourself, there's no shame in hiring a professional designer. But whether you decide to go it on your own or get professional assistance, the information in this section will help you consolidate your thoughts so you can express them clearly and get the garden you want.

BIG IDEAS

In this section you will broadly evaluate your goals as they pertain to your entire landscape. The process involves creating a sketch of your yard that includes spelling out what you want, where you want it, and what you can do about it. It will help you look at your garden with new eyes.

MAKE A BUBBLE PLAN

Begin by making a rough sketch called a bubble plan. This is the first step toward defining the areas in your yard that will come together to form the whole. What you're creating is equivalent to a writer's outline; a bubble plan helps you see the big picture while keeping track of the details.

On a piece of paper, draw an outline of your property along with the location of the house and other structures, paths, existing trees,

Rough out a simplified layout of your house and yard, showing trees, paths, and other existing hardscape elements.

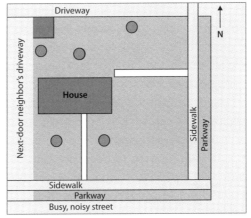

Add garden conditions and other things to consider.

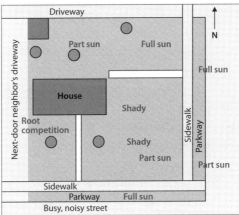

Define garden spaces and envision your ideal layout.

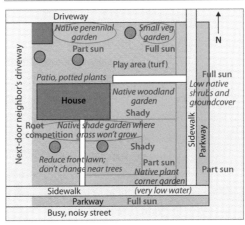

fences, doors, driveways, and other landmarks. It does not have to be very accurate—just get down the basics. You may want to make copies of this initial draft so you can draw different garden designs on them. The bubble plan will include both practicalities and dreams, so make it easy to erase so you can let yourself go crazy and experiment.

Next, annotate the plan with everything that comes to mind about your existing garden. Every yard has positive attributes that you'll want to take advantage of, but there are also negatives to keep in mind, since a good landscape plan can overcome some of them. Be sure to include things like lovely spots to sit and areas that can be seen from inside the house, and also note issues like ugly views and busy streets. Consider how a large telephone pole, street lamp, or building could be obscured with a tree or a pergola, and how the soothing sound of a bubbling fountain might mask the noise from neighbors or heavy traffic. Once you have spelled out the problems, creative thinking can provide the solutions.

Your garden plan should also include information on the overall growing conditions, including details about soil, exposure, and special elements like reflected heat from a wall, low points where water collects, and any other things that will impact your plants and how you use the space.

Now comes the fun part. What would you like to have in your yard? Think about what you want your garden to be and what you want to do in your yard. If you always dreamed of having a hot tub but cannot afford one, go ahead and draw one in. It doesn't cost anything to look, and you may even be able to design a less-expensive temporary solution that will make it easy to pop one in after you win the lottery. Do you want a vegetable or herb garden, or do you have a dog that needs a place to run? Will children be playing catch in the yard? Do you really need or want an expanse of water-guzzling lawn? Would you like trees to cool your house with energy-saving shade? Your garden plan can be a kind of wish list.

The next part requires a bit of honesty. In fact, the more honest you are, the happier you will be in the future. Ask yourself who is going to take care of the yard. Even if you are an avid gardener and would love

MY DREAMS FOR WILD SUBURBIA

- A healthy and relaxing oasis
- Habitat for lots of butterflies, lizards, and birds (especially hummingbirds)
- A highly sensory environment: interesting aromas, beautiful colors, natural sounds (no machine noise), tasty plants, and variable tactile experiences
- A safe place for grandchildren to play
- Sustainable maintenance, with little supplemental water and no poisons
- Fruit trees and a vegetable/herb garden
- Gardens, not lawn

MY REALITIES

- **Maintenance:** I will be doing most of the installation and maintenance, and I'm not getting any younger (although who is?). We travel a lot and can hire help if needed, but I do not want a "mow-and-blow" crew.
- **Neighborhood:** We live in a historic area in a small suburban town. Our house fronts on a busy street and is very close to a next-door neighbor, whose garage is on the property line.
- **Family:** My husband prefers some lawn area, and our grandchildren will play in the yard. We also have a dog.
- **Yard:** We have five mature trees (sixty years and older). One is native oak, the rest are exotic.

to spend every free moment weeding, digging, and getting dirty, how much time and energy can you realistically devote to it? Although you can dream big, as I have encouraged above, you must also be practical. If you do not have the desire or time to work in the garden and cannot afford to hire a gardener, design a low-maintenance yard.

Now, go back to your bubble plans and decide which ones look the most appealing and practical, which ones will best meet your needs and desires.

DON'T NEGLECT THE BIG PICTURE

As you debate various garden plans, remember to take a step back and consider the entire yard as a whole. Failing to take a holistic view may result in—as a designer once said of my garden—a hodgepodge rather than a coordinated landscape. This is especially true for those of us who do not have landscape design expertise.

As you plan your garden, try to develop a "big picture" landscape, or at least an image in your mind that you can work toward. Take photographs, make drawings, and keep looking at your yard from all angles. Take in the views from upstairs windows, across the street, the back yard, the front yard, out the kitchen window, through the entry gate, from every point of view you can get to. In fact, take a cup of coffee outside in the morning and a glass of wine in the evening so you can take in the scene at different times of day. Stop and look at the garden on your way to work; when you return home, pause for a moment, take a deep breath, and pay attention to what you see. Gardens should look good at all times of day, and they should please

The view of my front yard from my office.

from indoors as well as out. Create interesting vistas from windows in rooms you spend time in. Plan for the future. Ask your friends and family for ideas. If you are still flummoxed, seek professional help, but never stop looking and thinking.

DETAILS

Once you have done all of the above, you are ready to get out the tape measure and make an accurate, scaled plan of the area you will be landscaping. (It is not necessary to have a scaled plan for the entire yard.) I must confess that I do not always do this, but when I do, it is worth it. In addition to lending order to the garden design, it will help you avoid crowding, which is one of the most common design mistakes. You will also consider other important details that will help you get the garden you dream of. These include irrigation, your neighbors, rules and regulations, and general tips for designing a manageable yet beautiful garden.

DRAW A SCALED PLAN

The scaled plan should include the size of the beds and the location of all paths, irrigation, benches, and other permanent structures, also

A scaled plan of the parkway adjacent to my home.

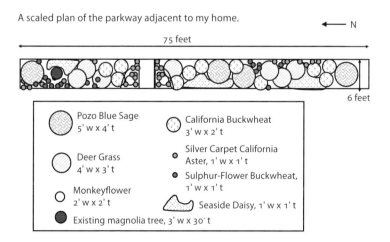

75 feet

6 feet

N

Pozo Blue Sage
5' w x 4' t

California Buckwheat
3' w x 2' t

Deer Grass
4' w x 3' t

Silver Carpet California
Aster, 1' w x 1' t

Sulphur-Flower Buckwheat,
1' w x 1' t

Monkeyflower
2' w x 2' t

Seaside Daisy, 1' w x 1' t

Existing magnolia tree, 3' w x 30' t

called *hardscape*. Include existing plants, particularly trees, that will remain in the garden. Then, draw in new paths, irrigation, borders, and any other design elements you hope to incorporate. Hardscape forms the bones of the garden and is difficult to change, so now is the time to get it right.

One way to go about this is to create a base plan—measured to scale—with all of the elements that exist and will remain in the garden, and then use tracing paper over that to show where you will make additions or alterations to the layout. Get out your colored pencils and sketch away! Show the flow of traffic through the garden. Draw in a bench and a birdbath. Do not hold back. Create as many tracing-paper sketches as you want.

CHOOSE YOUR IRRIGATION STYLE

Gardens landscaped with native plants adapted to local conditions use significantly less water than traditional lawn-dominated yards, and some will thrive—once established—with no supplemental water. However, many of the native perennials used in gardens are derived from species that get more water from natural sources (rain, fog, snow-melt) than may be available in your locale. For this reason, it is crucial to consider how much water your plants will need and how they will get it. Even if you are hoping to use mostly rainfall, you should still think about how you will water your new plantings while they are becoming established. The following is a brief overview beginning with the most sustainable systems—rain gardens and graywater—and moving on to standard irrigation methods. (For references on irrigation and rainwater harvesting, see Further Reading, starting on page 204.)

Rain gardens make use of natural rainwater-harvesting techniques. This may be as simple as diverting water from a downspout into a garden or rain barrel or as elaborate as a system that stores large amounts of runoff for use throughout the year. Many gardens today are being designed with dry streambeds (contoured gullies or basins often lined or filled with rocks). Water from downspouts or other places that may have previously emptied to the street and the storm drain system is directed into the dry streambeds. This design method provides additional groundwater for the garden while also reducing urban runoff. If building a rain garden sounds like something that might work for you, there are many resources with information specifically on these types of designs.

In addition to rainwater, water from clothes washers, showers, and sinks—referred to as *graywater*—can also be diverted for garden use. Again, there are important considerations if you plan to do this, so be sure to educate yourself first.

You can also, of course, water your garden the way your grandparents did: with an old-fashioned hose and nozzle or a portable sprinkler hooked up to a source of either potable or, if it is available to you, recycled water. This is an inexpensive, easy, and effective way to care for your new garden, especially if you are planning to let Mother Nature take over the watering tasks once the plants are established. Remember, however, that if you plan to use this lo-fi hand-watering system— whether for a couple of years or for the life of the garden—you will be babysitting your plants throughout the year. A mistimed vacation can cause significant losses, so keep that in mind.

There are many ways to deliver water to native plants, and there is much debate about the *best* way. Some garden experts reject the use of drip, low-volume, or inline drip emitters, all of which send water through small plastic tubing that leads to mini-sprinklers or drip holes delivering water directly to the root area of the plant. Although these systems are efficient, the water does not fall to the ground like natural rainfall, wetting the leaves of the plant in addition to the roots, and to some experts that makes these methods less than ideal. My feeling is that they are useful during establishment and, if they are designed to thoroughly wet the root zone and beyond to the proper depth, they can be effective.

Last but not least, there are the tried-and-true permanent, in-ground spray or rotor sprinkler systems. These require careful planning because they are difficult to modify once installed. As you design

IRRIGATION PROS AND CONS

Method	Description	Pros	Cons
Mother Nature	Water comes from rainfall, fog, snow, runoff, and other naturally occurring sources.	• Conserves water • Excellent water quality: neutral pH, low in salts and minerals • No setup expense	• Limits plant selection • Needs supplemental water for new plantings • May need supplemental water during drier parts of the year, especially in times of severe drought
Rainwater harvesting	Water from roofs and other non-permeable surfaces is directed to the garden. Some systems include storage facilities for later use of excess water.	• Conserves water • Excellent water quality • Directs more water to gardens • Reduces runoff • Can store water for later needs	• Storage tanks can be expensive • Must be done correctly to ensure it causes no flooding damage to structures • Requires planning and setup
Graywater	Water from showers, laundry machines, and sinks is diverted into the garden. This water can be applied with a drip system or by a hose.	• Conserves water • Available all year	• Water not as pure as potable water or rainwater • Must use appropriate soaps • Requires planning and setup

Method	Description	Pros	Cons
Hand-watering (sprinkler or hose)	The garden receives water from a hose via sprinklers or a hand-held nozzle.	• Can be highly efficient if you apply water to individual plants as needed • No setup expense	• Very time-consuming • More likely to lead to underwatering plants (you might not let the water thoroughly soak to the proper depth)
Drip/low-volume system	Water from a spigot is distributed through light plastic tubing with drip or low-volume emitters; an automatic controller can be attached.	• Efficient: directs water to individual plants • Easy to modify • Especially good for containers • Good for young plants during the establishment period • Can be programmed • Less expensive than more permanent systems	• Plastic tubing is easily damaged • Requires setup • Water delivery does not mimic natural rainfall, may encourage disease in natives, and doesn't wash off the leaves • Tubing and emitters may need to be moved as plants grow

(Table continued on the next page)

your sprinkler layout, be sure all of the plants in a given zone will have similar water needs in terms of amount and frequency, since you won't have a way to customize it for individual plants.

As with everything in gardening, there are pros and cons to each method. Consider the options, educate yourself, and select what will work best for you.

IRRIGATION PROS AND CONS *continued*

Method	Description	Pros	Cons
Inline emitters	Water is distributed through plastic tubing with evenly spaced holes. The system can be attached to a spigot with an automatic controller.	• Very efficient • Placement of surface tubing can be easily modified • Distributes water evenly if properly installed	• Buried lines are not easily moved or checked for damage; you might not know about problems until a plant shows stress or dies • Surface lines are easily damaged, and you might not know until a plant dies • If the lines are not placed properly, you can lose plants • Underground water delivery does not mimic natural rainfall, may encourage disease in natives, and doesn't wash off the leaves • Tubing may need to be moved as plants grow

CONSIDER THE NEIGHBORS

I would be remiss if I didn't mention another important issue: the neighbors. Keep in mind that if you are going for a bold approach to garden design, they may see your project as taking the neighborhood down a notch. This is especially true if you are new to the area. To

Method	Description	Pros	Cons
Permanent in-ground system, spray or rotors	Rotor or spray sprinkler heads are attached to an underground system of PVC pipes, usually designed with a controller that can water separate zones at different times and amounts.	• Distributes water evenly; especially appropriate for expanses of lawn • Durable, long-lasting • Easy to use if properly planned • Can be programmed • Overhead water delivery mimics natural rainfall	• Since it is easy to program and use, it can be wasteful if not set and managed appropriately; broken and misaligned sprinklers can be particularly wasteful • Overhead water can cause leaf spot on certain plants, especially in areas with high humidity or fog • Expensive to design and install • Difficult to modify as changes occur in the garden

some, bare dirt in the front yard, even as a temporary condition, is akin to outfitting your yard with a collection of old jalopies propped up on blocks.

If you are on speaking terms with your neighbors—and you really should be if you are going to embark on a major landscaping project—talk to them about what you are planning to do. Let them know it is going to be beautiful and environmentally friendly, and do it without heaping guilt on them for their own wasteful ways. Assure them that once you convert the now vacant lot of your front yard into a garden, you intend to maintain it. Tell them that they will be seeing butterflies and birds as the native plants become established. In fact, posting a sign informing walkers that your yard is in the process of becoming a native habitat is especially helpful. The National Wildlife Federation's

Above: A newly planted garden in Claremont, April 2005.
Below: Properly spaced Pigeon Point coyote brush, deer grass, and Canyon Prince giant wild rye filled out nicely by April 2007.

The Backyard Wildlife Habitat sign next to the sidewalk explains the environmental benefits of the parkway garden.

Certified Wildlife Habitat sign posted on my fence along the sidewalk garden is read and commented on by many passersby. It helps people know that the plants they may mistake for weeds are actually desired and desirable. And finally, consider that paths, benches, boulders, and steps help define a garden, whether it is native or not, and including these hardscape elements will not only enhance the look of your finished garden, they also make the garden approachable, usable, and understandable for those that visit it.

CHECK RULES AND REGULATIONS

So let's say you have decided on a plan and discussed it with your neighbors. Dare I ask at this point, did you check the rules and regulations of your city or homeowner association to make sure you are even *allowed* to remove your lawn? Anecdotal stories in Southern California from Lawndale, Glendale, and even my own city of South Pasadena suggest you take this issue seriously or be prepared to pay

DESIGN TIPS

- **Hardscape provides form and function.** Paths, benches, walls, decks, and other built elements not only have functionality but also define garden spaces and create flow and order in the garden. (For resources on hardscape, see Further Reading, starting on page 204.)

- **Take gardening hints from nature.** Go hiking to see what grows well in your area. Notice groupings of different plants and the conditions in which they thrive together.

- **Select plants compatible with your conditions and practices.** A well-designed garden is both beautiful and appropriate to your lifestyle; the plantings should look good, but they should also only demand as much maintenance as you are prepared to give them. For example, if you like a neat, tidy garden and dislike raking, do not use plants that perpetually drop leaves and debris.

- **Group plants with similar requirements.** *Hydrozoning* is the name for the common-sense practice of grouping plants with similar water needs. It saves time when hand-watering, as well as precious water. Pay attention to natural plant associations to gather information on which plants have similar needs.

- **Don't crowd your plants.** This is harder than you might think. When you pick up a one-gallon pot with a scrawny young plant in it, it can be hard to believe that in a relatively short time it

the price. With water shortages and other environmental concerns changing the way we think about landscaping, these ordinances and rules should be, and are in many cases, under serious review, but you can't always count on your city being as progressive as you are. Make your life easier and check first to see what you can and cannot do.

And now we are finally ready for the fun part: the plants! With more than six thousand to choose from, California natives offer beauty can grow to be fifteen feet wide. But if that's what the label says, believe it! Crowding plants is a common mistake.

- **Keep it simple but interesting.** There are so many great plants to choose from that sometimes it is hard limit oneself. Remember: groups of similar plants provide order that is more pleasing to the eye than a jumble, so although you should include enough variety to keep your garden interesting, don't get carried away. Fewer different types of plants will create a more calming look, and they will also be easier to maintain.

- **Mulch is your friend.** Mulch can reduce the amount of watering and weeding a garden requires, and it also gives a finished look to young gardens. (See "Mulch," on page 140, for more information.) Use woodchips or other organic mulches for a woodland appearance in wetter gardens, and gravel or other inorganic materials in dry gardens that reflect desert or chaparral conditions.

- **Remove troublesome plants.** Just because a plant is healthy does not mean you have to keep it. If it requires constant pruning because, for example, you planted it too close to a walkway, by all means get rid of it. If it is the wrong plant or in the wrong place, move it or remove it.

- **Relax and enjoy your garden.** If your garden is causing you stress and misery, you are doing something wrong. Relax and enjoy—after all, they are only plants!

and variety, so take your time finding exactly what you want. Unlike your hardscape design elements, the plants will—and should—change over time, so do not worry if you make some mistakes. Take it slow, knowing that you will get better at this as you go. The next main section will give you more specific advice on how to become familiar with the unusual and exciting California native plants that will feel right at home in your garden.

GARDEN INTERLUDE: BEFORE CONTACT

The parkway—the long narrow strip of ground between the street and the sidewalk—is my first major gardening project in my new home in California. I plan to replace the weedy grass with a garden that requires little or no irrigation. My low-maintenance native plant garden will also provide good habitat for wildlife, attracting birds, bees, and butterflies.

I know that to create a garden that will do well with little attention and resources, I must match the plants to the conditions. Therefore, I must know what I'm dealing with. Mature trees shade much of the yard, but the strip is quite sunny, and although I plan to set up a low-volume irrigation system for the young plants, in the long-term I hope to do away with irrigation altogether.

The next thing I look at is the soil, since easy gardening means plants and soil are compatible. I have lived in many places, but it is not until I put shovel to dirt that I feel at home. My first house as an adult had a garden in a hilly area with rocky soil, and working the land was a real challenge. Wherever I put the spade, I hit something hard and unyielding, and in my mind the subterranean rock took on the proportions of a boulder roughly the size of the iceberg that sunk the *Titanic*. As a child growing up on Long Island, I had loved digging for the small, rounded rocks made of quartz that were commonplace at the southern edge of the last glacial advance, but once I was responsible for a garden

This sprouted acorn is one of many in my yard. Several have grown into trees, including the lovely one shown opposite.

of my own, rocks were almost always a nuisance. Mercifully, my soil here in Southern California is rock-free, yet still well drained. Located far from the youthful, rapidly rising San Gabriel Mountains, the garden soil is made up of medium-sized particulates, neither clayey nor rocky.

As I start this garden project, I think about what may have grown here before the land became residential plots. This mindset helps me accomplish my main goals: creating a low-maintenance garden with high habitat value.

This heritage oak in my back yard grew from an acorn that sprouted more than sixty-five years ago.

Therefore, the question that hounds me here in urban California is, What plants used to live here before Europeans arrived? I do not know of any natural open space that still exists nearby, and, in fact, I do not even know of any rivers or creeks that in any way resemble their wild selves. Streams and creeks that once flowed here are mostly buried, though some still see daylight as they head toward the sea in concrete channels, more akin to sewage drains than natural waterways. Whenever I visit museums or libraries here, I look for pictures of the Los Angeles Basin. Mostly, it looks flat and dusty, with very little vegetation at all.

My garden, located in the flats of South Pasadena, is in the San Gabriel Valley, roughly six and a half miles south of the foothills of the San Gabriel Mountains, and twenty miles from the Pacific Ocean. I learn that the area was first developed at the turn of the century, and prior to residential development, this was a rich agricultural region, primarily lined with orange groves. For thousands of years before European settlement, the area was inhabited by an indigenous group known today as the Tongva, which loosely translates as "the people."

One day, while enjoying lunch with a colleague and friend, I asked her whether she had any knowledge of what used to grow here. She pointed out the obvious: street names here include Oak Street, Oak Knoll, Los Robles (Spanish for "The Oaks"), Dos Robles, Fair Oaks, Five Oaks Drive, Charter Oak Street, Oaklawn Avenue, and so on. Indeed, acorns sprout in my garden like they belong. In fact, the most beautiful and majestic tree in my yard is a volunteer oak that sprouted from an acorn about sixty years ago. A lightbulb goes on: this region was oak woodland!

With a picture in my mind of families of indigenous people working, playing, and eating among magnificent old oaks, I set to work on my parkway. Aromatic sages, delicate bunchgrasses, and cheerful wildflowers will be planted between three widely spaced coast live oaks. Over time the oaks will grow and mature, shading out the understory plants, and as I grow older and less able to bend and weed, the oaks will provide shade and comfort in a carefree garden space. I am taking care of the garden so one day it will be able to take care of itself.

LEARN ABOUT NATIVE PLANTS

I F YOU ARE new to gardening with California native plants, you might be feeling a bit overwhelmed. There are a lot of resources offering a lot of information and advice, and you might feel like you're in over your head. But fear not: in this chapter I will familiarize you with twenty common natives that are among the easiest to grow of the myriad wild plants you might choose from. They are generally available in the trade, amendable to the modified conditions of our gardens, and exceptionally beautiful. Among them are trees, various sizes of shrubs (large, medium-sized, and low-growing), herbaceous perennials, and one vine. Following the information on these plants, you'll find a detailed list of other ways to learn about what native plants might work in your garden.

TOP TWENTY

Tall: Over 6 feet
1. Western Sycamore
2. Coast Live Oak
3. Desert Museum Palo Verde
4. Toyon
5. Common Manzanita
6. Ray Hartman California Lilac

Medium: 3 to 6 feet
7. Howard McMinn Manzanita
8. Golden Abundance Barberry
9. Coffeeberry
10. Palmer's Mallow
11. Cleveland Sage
12. Deer Grass

Low: Under 3 feet
13. Yankee Point California Lilac
14. Creeping Barberry
15. Bee's Bliss Sage
16. Margarita BOP Penstemon
17. California Fuchsia
18. Coral Bells
19. Catalina Island Live-Forever

Vine
20. Roger's Red Grape

Western sycamores on a beautiful residential street.

Fruits dangle in a chain.

1. WESTERN SYCAMORE

Platanus racemosa

Plant form: Tree, deciduous

Average size: 40–90 ft. tall

Flower color: No petals; red stigmas on female flowers in spring

Berries/fruit: Several balls of seeds hang like dangling earrings

Exposure: Full sun

Water needs: Moderate; roots of mature trees may have reached groundwater

Soil type: Adaptable

Ecology: Riparian, woodland

Habitat value: Birds and butterflies; hummingbirds use leaf fluff to soften their nests

Comments: Though this tree drops leaves and can be messy, it grows fast and will give your garden a refreshing riparian ambiance.

Male, pollen-bearing flowers.

Autumn color.

Female flowers.

Whitish, angular trunks of deciduous sycamores draw attention in winter.

This oak provides cooling shade, and its gray trunk is a focal point.

2. COAST LIVE OAK
Quercus agrifolia
Plant form: Tree, evergreen
Average size: 40 ft. tall and wide
Flower color: Inconspicuous
Berries/fruit: Acorn
Exposure: Full sun to part shade
Water needs: Low; no summer watering needed for mature specimens
Soil type: Adaptable; less susceptible to root rot in well-drained soils
Ecology: Oak woodland, chaparral
Habitat value: One mature tree is a habitat in itself and creates its own microclimate for birds, insects, and other creatures

Catkins are the male, pollen-producing flowers.

Acorn.

This oak sapling, planted in Pasadena, will grow faster than one might expect.

This magnificent oak predates the neighborhood's development.

Comments: This tree grows faster than most would guess. In ten to fifteen years it can reach twenty feet in height and provide cooling shade. Once established, avoid summer watering to discourage root fungus. Future generations will thank you for planting an oak.

A lovely multi-trunked oak in a local park.

3. DESERT MUSEUM PALO VERDE

Showy flowers.

Parkinsonia 'Desert Museum'
Plant form: Tree, drought deciduous
Average size: 25 ft. tall and wide
Flower color: Yellow
Berries/fruit: Inconspicuous
Exposure: Full sun
Water needs: Low; accepts some summer watering
Soil type: Prefers well-drained soils
Ecology: Desert
Habitat value: Bees

The tree in heavy bloom in late May at Rancho Santa Ana Botanic Garden.

Expect blooms in spring and summer.

Comments: This fast-growing, thornless hybrid blooms profusely in spring and summer. Large black bumblebees are especially attracted to its flowers. Avoid using in windy sites, since brittle branches break easily.

Bees, especially large bumblebees, find this flower irresistible.

Some people claim that Hollywood was named for the red-berried toyons that reminded newcomers of the holly bushes common in the East.

A syrphid fly on toyon flowers, which attract various pollinators when they bloom in summer.

Berries vary in color from brilliant red to orange and yellow.

4. TOYON

Heteromeles arbutifolia

Plant form: Shrub/tree, evergreen

Average size: 8–15 ft. tall and 15 ft. wide

Flower color: White

Berries/fruit: Clusters of berries, usually red, but sometimes yellow or orange

Exposure: Full sun to part shade

Water needs: Low

Soil type: Adaptable

Ecology: Oak woodland, riparian, chaparral, coastal sage scrub

Clusters of red berries against the dark green leaves of the toyon in the late autumn give this sidewalk garden a festive holiday appeal.

Habitat value: Berries eaten by birds

Comments: Allow this adaptable evergreen to grow naturally, or prune it to be a single- or multi-trunked tree or a hedge. Its red berries make a perfect winter holiday decoration.

In my garden, toyon acts as a screen and provides bright autumn color.

Toyon growing in my partly shaded garden.

Yellow toyon berries from the Davis Gold cultivar in Rancho Santa Ana Botanic Garden.

Bark glistens in the sunlight after a rain.

Dangling bell-shaped flowers appear in late winter to early spring.

5. COMMON MANZANITA

Arctostaphylos manzanita and cultivars

Plant form: Tree/shrub, evergreen

Average size: 10–12 ft. tall and wide

Flower color: White to pinkish-white

Berries/fruit: Light-colored berries turning red-brown as they mature

Exposure: Full sun to part shade

Water needs: Low

Soil type: Prefers well-drained soils

Ecology: Chaparral

Habitat value: Bees

A common manzanita at Rancho Santa Ana Botanic Garden.

The manzanita's angular branching upright habit and rich, smooth, brown bark make this a striking garden shrub or tree.

Comments: The smooth, sinuous branches of this large shrub or small tree are covered with attractive cinnamon-brown bark that begs to be stroked.

A specimen at the Tree of Life Nursery.

Flower clusters are three to four inches in length.

6. RAY HARTMAN CALIFORNIA LILAC

Ceanothus 'Ray Hartman'

Plant form: Shrub, evergreen

Average size: 12–18 ft. tall and wide

Flower color: Blue

Berries/fruit: Three-lobed fruits; not showy

Exposure: Full sun to part shade

Water needs: Low to moderate; accepts some summer watering

Soil type: Prefers well-drained soils; accepts heavier garden soils

Ecology: Chaparral

Habitat value: Bees

Comments: Ray Hartman is the oldest and one of the most reliable ceanothus cultivars. It is deep green year round, with a striking springtime display of blue flowers.

Glossy green leaves with clusters of blue flowers make this an exceptional shrub in spring.

Deep-blue flowers contrast with the nearby bright-orange California poppies.

This fast-growing shrub can reach six feet in height and width in just a few years.

Light pink flowers appear in late winter.

The name "manzanita" is derived from the Spanish word for "little apples," referring to this plant's small red berries.

7. HOWARD MCMINN MANZANITA

Arctostaphylos 'Howard McMinn'
Plant form: Tree/shrub, evergreen
Average size: 6–8 ft. tall and wide
Flower color: Light pink
Berries/fruit: Berries when ripe look like tiny red apples
Exposure: Full sun to part shade
Water needs: Low to moderate
Soil type: Adaptable; prefers well-drained soils
Ecology: Chaparral
Habitat value: Birds and bees
Comments: This dependable shrub is a garden favorite due to its lovely smooth, dark-red bark and its profusion of soft, pink, bell-shaped flowers in early spring.

An older specimen at Rancho Santa Ana Botanic Garden.

This five-year-old shrub blooms profusely.

Manzanita planted as a hedge at the Theodore Payne Foundation.

Clusters of yellow flowers in mid-spring.

Blue berries appear
late summer to fall.

8. GOLDEN ABUNDANCE BARBERRY

Berberis 'Golden Abundance'

Plant form: Tree/shrub, evergreen

Average size: 5–8 ft. tall and 6–12 ft. wide

Flower color: Yellow

Berries/fruit: Blue berries

Exposure: Full sun to part shade

Water needs: Low to moderate; accepts some summer watering

Soil type: Adaptable

Ecology: Chaparral, woodland

Habitat value: Birds and bees

Comments: This plant looks beautiful every season, with its showy yellow flowers in spring, blue berries in summer, occasional bright-red leaves in winter, and shiny holly-like leaves throughout the year.

Yellow flowers contrast with red stems and glossy, dark-green leaves.

This hedge stands out against the light-green wall.

The flowering shrub in early spring.

Inconspicuous cream flowers attract bees and form next year's berries.

A foundation shrub in my front yard.

9. COFFEEBERRY

Frangula californica and cultivars

Plant form: Tree/shrub, evergreen

Average size: 3–12 ft. tall, depending on cultivar

Flower color: Cream

Berries/fruit: Red, brown, and deep-purple berries

Exposure: Full sun to part shade

Water needs: Low

Soil type: Adaptable

Ecology: Woodland, chaparral, coastal sage scrub

This store is landscaped with coffeeberry shrubs beneath a western sycamore.

Habitat value: Birds and bees
Comments: Coffeeberry is a neat and durable shrub with evergreen leaves and pretty red to deep-purple berries. It can be pruned as a hedge or allowed to grow naturally.

As coffeeberries ripen, they darken from light yellow to nearly black in color.

A blooming shrub at the Prisk School-yard Habitat Garden in Long Beach.

10. PALMER'S MALLOW

Abutilon palmeri

Plant form: Shrub, semi-evergreen

Average size: 4–5 ft. tall and wide

Flower color: Yellow

Berries/fruit: Ornamental seed capsules

Exposure: Full sun to some afternoon shade

Water needs: Low

Soil type: Prefers well-drained soils

Ecology: Desert, coastal sage scrub

Habitat value: Birds (especially hummingbirds) and bees

Comments: Few plants bloom as much as this one. Its yellow-orange flowers stand out against a background of velvety gray leaves.

A yellow flower on soft gray leaves.

Mallows have reseeded in the front yard of this private garden.

This plant has been in its pot for over five years. It blooms several times a year.

Palmer's mallow in my front yard.

A seed capsule.

Palmer's mallow in a private home on the Theodore Payne Foundation Garden Tour.

This unusual selection made at Rancho Santa Ana Botanic Garden was named for salvia expert Betsy Clebsch. Its flowers are white and blue, varying within and among clusters.

A recently planted Winnifred Gilman sage blooms in May at Rancho Santa Ana Botanic Garden.

11. CLEVELAND SAGE

Salvia clevelandii and cultivars

Plant form: Herbaceous, semi-evergreen

Average size: 3–5 ft. tall and wide

Flower color: Purple, blue, or rarely white

Berries/fruit: Inconspicuous

Exposure: Full sun

Water needs: Low; no summer watering

Soil type: Prefers well-drained soils

Its deep-purple flowers and compact size make the Winnifred Gilman an excellent plant for dry gardens with full sun and well-drained soils.

The purple-and-white flowers of the Betsy Clebsch Cleveland sage.

A spectacular bloom in late spring in my parkway garden.

In late July, the plant goes dormant, dropping most of its leaves. Supplemental water may pull it out of dormancy, but that risks the plant rotting from too much summer moisture.

Ecology: Coastal sage scrub
Habitat value: Birds (especially hummingbirds) and bees
Comments: People walking past this small gray shrub always stop to locate the source of the sweet-spicy aroma it exudes. In spring it is covered with rich violet-blue flowers. Plant it in a hot, dry garden.

Repetition is comforting to the eye at Rancho Santa Ana Botanic Garden. From bottom to top: white sage, deer grass, Pigeon Point coyote brush in front of the building, and Russian River wild grape on the trellis.

These bunchgrasses gracefully drape over the smooth boulder and provide interesting textural variation to nearby shrubs.

12. DEER GRASS

Muhlenbergia rigens

Plant form: Grass, perennial

Average size: 3 ft. tall and 4 ft. wide

Flower color: Buff

Berries/fruit: Inconspicuous

Exposure: Full sun to part shade

A partly shaded garden at Rancho Santa Ana Botanic Garden.

Deer grass in my parkway garden.

Water needs: Low; accepts summer watering
Soil type: Adaptable
Ecology: Woodland, coastal sage scrub, grassland
Habitat value: Food for birds and insects

Comments: This long-living, easy-to-grow bunchgrass looks especially nice with boulders. It is buff-colored in winter and green in summer.

The Prisk Schoolyard Habitat Garden in Long Beach.

Yankee Point groundcover with red-berried toyons in the front yard of a private residence in Los Angeles.

13. YANKEE POINT CALIFORNIA LILAC

Ceanothus thyrsiflorus
var. *griseus* 'Yankee Point'
Plant form: Low shrub or
groundcover, evergreen
Average size: 2–3 ft. tall
(can grow taller in advanced
age) and 8–10 ft. wide

Flower color: Blue
Berries/fruit: Three-lobed
fruits; not showy
Exposure: Sun, part shade,
or shade
Water needs: Low
Soil type: Adaptable

Draping over a wall at Rancho Santa Ana Botanic Garden.

Ecology: Coastal sage scrub
Habitat value: Birds and bees
Comments: This durable
groundcover will mound up
if planted too close together.
When given proper spacing,
the only pruning required is to
remove the occasional upright
stems to maintain low growth.

Glossy, dark-green leaves
and clusters of blue flowers.

This old specimen at Rancho Santa Ana Botanic Garden has striking blue-gray leaves.

Clusters of yellow flowers in mid-spring.

14. CREEPING BARBERRY

Berberis aquifolium var. *repens*

Plant form: Low shrub or groundcover, evergreen

Average size: 1–3 ft. tall, spreading

Flower color: Yellow

Berries/fruit: Clusters of blue berries

Exposure: Part shade to shade

Water needs: Low to moderate; accepts some summer watering

Soil type: Adaptable

Creeping barberry growing under a mature oak in part shade.

Ecology: Woodland
Habitat value: Birds and bees
Comments: If you want a low-growing shrub for placement near an oak or other tree, this drought-tolerant barberry, with its showy yellow flowers in spring, will fit the bill.

Though this plant is evergreen, some of its leaves turn bright red and drop in autumn.

Bee's Bliss sage grows around flowering Golden Abundance barberry.

In spring, lavender blooms attract pollinators.

15. BEE'S BLISS SAGE

Salvia 'Bee's Bliss'

Plant form: Groundcover, evergreen

Average size: 1–2 ft. tall and 6–8 ft. wide

Flower color: Lavender

Berries/fruit: Inconspicuous

Exposure: Full sun

Water needs: Low

Soil type: Prefers well-drained soils

Ecology: Coastal sage scrub

Habitat value: Birds (especially hummingbirds) and bees

Comments: Use this fast-growing gray-green groundcover in sunny locations.

It is susceptible to powdery
mildew, so avoid placement
in moist or damp gardens and
areas with overhead irrigation.

Groundcover planted in December
2004 at Rancho Santa Ana Botanic
Garden.

One year after planting, Bee's Bliss
sage (foreground) and Frosty Dawn
ceanothus have filled in around the
sculpture.

Growing in full sun, these flowers provide spectacular color in spring and a neat habitat the rest of the year.

Showy flowers change color from blue to violet with pink highlights.

16. MARGARITA BOP PENSTEMON

Penstemon heterophyllus 'Margarita BOP'

Plant form: Herbaceous perennial, evergreen

Average size: 1–3 ft. tall and 1–2 ft. wide

Flower color: Bright blue, purplish, or pink

Berries/fruit: Seeds

Exposure: Prefers full sun

Water needs: Low to moderate; accepts some summer watering

Yellow flower buds add to the array of spring colors.

Soil type: Adaptable
Ecology: Coastal sage scrub, chaparral, grassland
Habitat value: Bees, birds (especially hummingbirds), and butterflies

Comments: This is a perfect plant for new gardens. It blooms in its first year and fills in quickly.

In July at the cultivar bed at Rancho Santa Ana Botanic Garden, red blooms of California fuchsias are set off by purple sage and flowering California buckwheat.

17. CALIFORNIA FUCHSIA

Epilobium species and cultivars

Plant form: Herbaceous to subshrub, semi-evergreen

Cultivar field tests at Rancho Santa Ana Botanic Garden in September illustrate variation in size, foliage, flower color, and bloom period.

Average size: From less than 1 ft. up to 4 ft. tall, depending on cultivar

Flower color: Usually red, but can be pink or white

Berries/fruit: Seeds

Exposure: Full sun

Water needs: Low

Soil type: Prefers well-drained soils

Ecology: Chaparral, coastal sage scrub, grassland

Habitat value: Bees, birds (especially hummingbirds), and butterflies

Comments: Include California fuchsia in your garden to provide color during late summer and fall, when little else blooms. The hummingbirds will thank you.

California fuchsia growing on a roadside in the San Gabriel Mountains.

Red flowers brighten a dry, rocky slope in October.

A bee "steals" nectar without pollinating the flower.

Coral bells blooming with Pacific Coast hybrid irises at Rancho Santa Ana Botanic Garden in May.

18. CORAL BELLS

Heuchera species and cultivars

Plant form: Herbaceous, evergreen

Average size: From several inches to 2 ft. tall and wide, depending on cultivar

Flower color: White and shades of pink

Berries/fruit: Inconspicuous

Exposure: Full sun to part shade

Water needs: Moderate; needs summer watering

Soil type: Adaptable

Ecology: Woodland, riparian

Habitat value: Birds (especially hummingbirds) and bees

Comments: This perennial can be massed as a groundcover or grown in containers. Its long, delicate stems of flowers make romantic bouquets.

Wendy coral bells blooming in May at Rancho Santa Ana Botanic Garden.

Several coral bell varieties in containers in my backyard garden.

Coral bells blooming at a private residence in Claremont.

Two popular cultivars: darker Genevieve on the left, light-pink Wendy on the right.

A groundcover of Catalina Island live-forever (in front) and coral bells (behind) grow under an oak tree at Rancho Santa Ana Botanic Garden.

19. CATALINA ISLAND LIVE-FOREVER

Dudleya virens ssp. *hassei*
Plant form: Succulent groundcover, evergreen
Average size: To 6 in. tall
Flower color: White
Berries/fruit: Inconspicuous
Exposure: Sun, part shade, or shade
Water needs: Low

Live-forever blooming in a container

Live-forever under a desert willow at Rancho Santa Ana Botanic Garden.

Soil type: Prefers good drainage but tolerates heavier garden soils

Ecology: Coastal sage scrub

Habitat value: Birds (especially hummingbirds) and bees

Comments: This durable live-forever forms a rosette of succulent gray leaves and can be used as a groundcover or as a container plant.

Live-forever among rocks in shade with wire grass and irises.

Autumn color in December in the Cultivar Garden at Rancho Santa Ana Botanic Garden.

20. ROGER'S RED GRAPE

Vitis 'Roger's Red'

Plant form: Vine, deciduous

Average size: Climbs to 25–40 ft. tall

Flower color: Inconspicuous, cream

Berries/fruit: Dark-purple grapes

Exposure: Part shade to shade

Water needs: Moderate, needs summer watering

Soil type: Adaptable

I'll run the ripe grapes I collected in August through a Foley mill to make a sweet and delicious juice.

Ecology: Riparian, woodland
Habitat value: Bees, birds, and squirrels
Comments: The bright-red autumn leaves of this vigorous vine will catch everyone's attention. It needs room and may require pruning due to its vigorous growth. The small grapes are tasty, but you will have to compete with the birds to get them.

Bright-red autumn foliage makes Roger's Red grape an amazing addition to gardens.

In mid-summer, the grapes start to ripen.

By January the leaves have fallen and revealed the twisted trunk of this woody vine.

HOW TO DISCOVER MORE NATIVE PLANTS

Although the twenty plants I just described are all excellent choices, there are literally hundreds of other natives that can adorn California gardens, providing beauty, sustainability, and habitat. The following suggestions will help you delve more deeply into the wonderful world of California native plants for the garden.

- Visit gardens that specialize in native plants
- Attend native plant garden tours
- Go to nurseries and plant sales that specialize in natives
- Take classes and attend talks
- Join garden clubs and other environmental organizations
- Peruse online resources
- Read books
- Hike local open spaces
- Walk the neighborhood
- Ask an expert

VISIT GARDENS THAT SPECIALIZE IN NATIVE PLANTS

Botanical gardens, native plant nurseries, and parks with sustainable, low-water-use displays have gardens featuring native plants. It is especially helpful to see examples of these plants as mature specimens growing in garden settings instead of only as young potted plants. (For a list of native plant gardens in Southern California, see Appendix C, starting on page 197.)

ATTEND NATIVE PLANT GARDEN TOURS

Cities, garden clubs, and native plant organizations often hold native plant garden tours in the spring. Gardeners enjoy sharing informa-

The floriforous groundcover of a seaside daisy cultivar.

tion on installation and maintenance, and they often label plants and provide plant lists to visitors. Remember, however, that you are seeing these gardens at their best. If possible, visit in the winter and summer as well, to see them when not in full bloom.

GO TO NURSERIES AND PLANT SALES THAT SPECIALIZE IN NATIVES

Many native plant groups hold plant sales as fundraisers, and knowledgeable volunteers and staff are on hand to answer questions. Nurseries that specialize in native plants are another excellent source of both plants and information. Although big-box stores and large commercial nurseries sometimes sell native plants, sales staff are not always informed on best horticultural practices for natives. (For a list of native plant nurseries in Southern California, see Appendix D, starting on page 199.)

TAKE CLASSES AND ATTEND TALKS

Water agencies, cities, botanical gardens, and native plant nurseries and organizations offer classes on sustainable gardening with native plants.

Small, tight mounds of David's Choice sandhill sagebrush blend in color with the blue-green Canyon Prince giant wild rye behind them.

JOIN GARDEN CLUBS AND OTHER ENVIRONMENTAL ORGANIZATIONS

Local clubs and groups offer volunteer opportunities, tours, trips, and other activities related to native plants and gardening. Since it is best to learn from people who are doing the same thing in the same area, these groups are an excellent resource for information relevant to your region.

PERUSE ONLINE RESOURCES

Check the Internet for information on native plants, while keeping in mind that there may be regional differences in plant-care suggestions. Also, there is no filter on the Internet, so you are likely to come across some contradictory and erroneous information. Blogs can provide personal experience, while websites of botanical gardens, universities, native plant nurseries, and environmental nonprofits are likely to have accurate materials.

The California Native Plant Society has recently implemented an online service called Calscape (http://calscape.cnps.org/) to help gardeners select native plants. Type in your home address, and the site will generate a list of native plants appropriate to your location. Be aware, however, that although the plants listed may be locally native, some may not be appropriate for your specific garden. This resource is a good starting point, but you will still need to choose plants based on the sun, soil, and water factors of your planting space. (For a list of online resources, see page 208.)

READ BOOKS

More books than ever are being published on "green" gardening. Their emphases vary from water conservation, water harvesting, habitat creation, native plants, and other sustainable practices. (For a list of books on sustainable and native plant gardening, see Further Reading, starting on page 204.)

HIKE LOCAL OPEN SPACES

Seeing native plants in their natural habitats is the best way to get to know them, so get out and enjoy hiking locally during all seasons of the year. In Southern California it may be difficult to find low-elevation coastal sage scrub, grassland, and oak woodland habitats, since nearly all of these regions have been developed, yet there is a wealth of foothill, coastal, desert, and high-elevation areas to explore.

WALK THE NEIGHBORHOOD

Seek out local gardens that incorporate some of the plants and practices that interest you. Gardeners love to talk about their gardens.

ASK AN EXPERT

Hire a landscape professional who specializes in native plant gardens.

GARDEN INTERLUDE:
A WILD PARKWAY

Walking on a quiet street in my Los Angeles suburb, my eighty-year-old father and I approach a lovely adobe home. After a few moments, I notice that he is slowly shaking his head. "It's not for me," he says. I am showing him a garden in my neighborhood that I am especially fond of. Paths wind through trees, shrubs, boulders, and benches in this small, lawnless yard. The plants and the look are a bit dry—Californian. My father, who grew up in New York City and raised his family in the suburbs, was accustomed to a lusher, neater look. I should not be surprised by his opinion, but I am. This garden serves as a model for what I want in my yard. It is natural and quiet, yet full of life. It reminds me of the nearby mountains I so love.

I live in a prim suburban neighborhood, and so I wonder whether my new parkway garden—on a prominent corner of a busy residential street—will be too wild for its surrounds. I am excited to think that my garden will reflect the naturally occurring vegetation that was here before development: oak trees interspersed with coastal sage scrub plants. Oaks grow on parkways throughout the area, so they will fit right in, but what will people think of the wild sage, buckwheat, and bunchgrass that will replace the tidy but boring green lawn? Sage scrub plants will do well in the dry, sunny garden, but they can look a bit unkempt. I will sow wild-flower seeds so springtime will be colorful, and I know that people will appreciate the butterflies as they gently glide along the sidewalk before alighting on the flowers of these wild plants. But what will people say of this garden when few plants are in bloom and many are dormant?

My reservations will not stop me. I am determined to give this a try, but I will take steps to communicate both what the garden is and why I have planted it. I will post attractive signs explaining that this is a low-water-use habitat garden. Since it is a parkway, I will put in flagstone paths from the sidewalk to the street. The paths both will make it easier for people to

Dudleyas, wild irises, and other Mediterranean plants create an artful
arrangement with rocks and logs.

Native grasses grow around boulders in the front yard of this
natural garden near my home.

traverse the garden and will serve as another indication that it is a planned
space, not a neglected one. I will take special care to prune any branches
that encroach on the walk and street, not just for safety but, again, to let
people know that this garden, though somewhat wild, is tended and main-
tained. I wonder whether these steps will be enough to get my father to
admit he sees beauty in my wild suburbia.

CREATE YOUR GARDEN

A T LAST WE are ready to put on our work clothes and get into the garden. This section starts with guidance on how to remove lawn in preparation for planting, and it then moves on to the installation of paths, benches, irrigation, and other hardscape elements that were discussed in the planning section. Irrigation and hardscape are beyond the scope of this book, but you can find many resources and professionals who can help you with those elements.

The fun continues to build as we finally get to visit nurseries to select plants. In this chapter I give tips to help you select strong and healthy specimens. After you have your plans and plants, you will be ready to dig in. Planning and prep may be the hard work, but planting, surely, is the fun! This section includes suggestions on how to plant properly, so you can give your new, young plants a good start in your garden. And finally, I offer a few pointers on ways to make the new garden look lush and full even when it's just starting out.

REMOVE THE LAWN

To make way for native garden beds in a yard covered with turf grass, the first step is to remove the lawn. Most old California lawns are a mix of Bermuda, St. Augustine, and sometimes kikiyu grass, along with a healthy crop of weeds. These are the plants that have survived for years, beating out the carefully and expensively laid sod grasses such as Marathon, EZ Hybrid Turf, and Harmony Home. Getting rid of this blanket of undesirables is no easy task. In this section we will cover the five basic approaches.

MECHANICAL REMOVAL

Mechanical removal is simple enough. You get out a spade and start digging, or you rent, purchase, or borrow a nifty device called a sod cutter, a machine sort of like a lawn mower that mows underground rather than above. Either way, mechanical removal is not for the weak of back. This is the method I have used most, so I am intimately familiar with its pluses and minuses, and make no mistake: it is hard work! If you have a teenager who is willing and able to help out with this, you're in luck. Otherwise, consider hiring some strong young bodies, or substitute this activity for several hours in the gym.

A big drawback to this method has to do with weeds. Digging creates a high level of disturbance in the soil, and weeds love disturbed conditions. Even the most meticulous digger will have to control for weeds in years to come. Definitely avoid rototilling yards that have been covered with Bermuda or kikiyou grass. The rototiller chops the stems and roots and replants them in the overturned soil, giving these noxious weeds ideal conditions to start growing again.

Also note that when you dig out the lawn, you inevitably remove some nice topsoil. But if you shake out the mat of turf to return as much soil to the garden as you can, you will deposit weed seeds, stems, and roots along with it. You can sieve the topsoil to separate the weedy stems and roots, but this is very time consuming. Your goal is to leave as much topsoil behind while also removing weedy propagules that may be enmeshed in the soil.

You must also decide what to do with the waste turf, and it's not as simple as tossing it in a compost pile. If you choose to compost it, as I did before I knew better, remember that many seeds and stems will survive and grow into weeds wherever you spread the compost. It may be better to put the old turf in the green-waste bin, with the hope that your local composting facility gets hot enough to destroy the weeds.

On the plus side, with this method you can dig and plant in the same day, a big advantage for the more spontaneous, or should I say impulsive, gardeners. Also, there is no financial cost associated with digging, unless you hire help, rent or buy a sod cutter, or need physical therapy for your aching back.

I have used this method because my yard has something I call "retreating lawn syndrome," a condition marked by the mysterious "retreat" of turf grass as bordering garden beds invade the lawn. In fact, every time my husband is out of town for a few days, my lawn retreats a bit. Whatever the cause of this enigma (wink, wink), it has allowed me to gradually extend beds of drought-tolerant plants while still maintaining a bit of grass to walk and play on. I know of no other way to perform this small-scale guerrilla attack on my lawn without the use of a shovel.

SUFFOCATION BY MULCH

Turf grass, like most plants, needs sunlight to grow. Depriving the lawn of sunlight by covering it with a thick layer of mulch is an effective way to kill your grass so you can plant a native garden in its place. As the mulch decomposes, it generates heat, which further facilitates decomposition of the grass.

I put this method to the test when a major windstorm hit our region and tree limbs came crashing down in our yard. Rather than having the branches carted away, I asked our arborist to chip the wood, which I then spread over half of our front lawn. Within six months the lawn was gone and a loamy layer of soil replaced it. Very little weeding has been required in subsequent years.

This method also increases the organic material in the soil, which is helpful for plants with high nutrient requirements, like edible vegetables. Many California native plants, however, grow best in leaner, well-drained soils. If you are planning to plant a desert- or chaparral-type garden, you may not want the rich, organic soil created as the mulch decomposes, since it can cause some dryland plants to rot or to grow so quickly that they may not be able to sustain their lush greenery when the weather turns hot and dry.

There has been a lot of discussion, especially among gardeners interested in sustainable practices, about a method called sheet mulching. In this method you mow the lawn low and then cover it with overlapping layers of biodegradable materials such as newspaper or

Broken limbs and downed trees were scattered throughout the neighborhood.

The woodchips from the debris were spread in a four-inch-thick layer. Within six months the lawn had decomposed beneath the mulch, leaving behind rich, organic soil.

cardboard. Next you moisten the soil and sheets thoroughly and cover them with a layer of organic mulch.

Some horticulturists, like Linda Chalker-Scott of the Garden Professors blog, contend that sheet mulching is no more effective than a four-to-six-inch layer of plain mulch, and, in fact, it can be less effective if the mulch slides or blows off the slippery surface of the cardboard. Another possible problem with this method is that the layer of cardboard itself reduces air and water exchange at the surface of the soil, certainly more so than just a layer of mulch alone. If you are sheet mulching a lawn area that is beneath or close to a large tree, you can create conditions in which disease-causing organisms thrive in the soil and endanger this nearby specimen. In spite of these warnings, however, I know of many gardeners, both professionals and hobbyists, who swear by this method.

However you do it, mulching to rid your yard of grass has many advantages. It is less backbreaking than digging the lawn out, and it doesn't take as long as straightforward neglect. If done neatly, a uniform surface of organic mulch will give your garden a tidy, finished look. Over time, it creates a layer of rich soil, which can nourish woodland or riparian plants (but potentially cause problems for desert or chaparral plants and also possibly exacerbate weed problems). Having a garden plan can help you decide if mulching is right for you.

SOLARIZATION

The sun can be a very effective weapon in your battle against lawn. This method, called *solarization,* is best for large, flat, sunny areas. Mow the lawn low to the ground, then dig a trench around the future garden bed. Soak the doomed lawn with water and then carefully and tightly position clear plastic sheeting over the surface. Try not to compact the wet soil by walking on it. Cover the edges of the tightly pulled plastic with the soil you dug out while making the trench.

Plastic sheeting tightly covers the moistened ground.

Although it may seem counterintuitive, clear plastic is generally more effective than the opaque black variety. Although darker colors do absorb heat, with the black plastic it is the sheeting, rather than the soil, that gets hot; with clear plastic, the sunlight shines through the sheeting, warming the soil and water beneath. That said, black plastic may work better than clear in cooler, less sunny areas, where the opacity of the material can keep weeds from photosynthesizing. Choose what works best for you.

In any case, employ this method during the hottest time of the year, leaving the plastic in place for several weeks. Thin plastic (1–2 mm) results in hotter temperatures at the surface than thicker plastic, but make sure the sheeting you use is also strong and resistant to ultraviolet light. Appropriate sheeting can be found in hardware, garden, or lumber stores.

Although it is heat that eradicates the weeds, the method is far from perfect, so use it thoughtfully. In addition to killing your lawn, hot steam may also kill soil bacteria and fungi, and it doesn't distinguish between the kinds that cause disease and those that are beneficial to plants. Also, the inhospitable conditions created on the surface would be detrimental to the roots of trees or shrubs that may be growing nearby. Furthermore, solarization does not always destroy seeds with strong seed coats or deeply buried stems of rhizomonous grasses. This method is labor-intensive, must be done well to work effectively, and can be expensive (although unused sheeting can be stored for future use). It is not fool-proof, but it can get the job done if conditions are right.

POISON

Many gardeners who wish to remove large areas of lawn opt for a fast and effective approach: poison. Glyphosate is the most common herbicide used by home gardeners and can be found in trademarked products with familiar names like Roundup, Doomsday, and Killzall. Plants absorb glyphosate through their leaves, and it kills them systemically. Once it has done its job, the poison quickly breaks down into byproducts that chemical companies assure us are nontoxic.

A large area at Rancho Santa Ana Botanic Garden is solarized in preparation for the sowing of annual wildflowers.

Since glyphosate destroys any plant it touches, apply it with care and never on windy days. For this herbicide to work, the target plants must be actively growing, so if you are trying to get rid of a warm-season grass, like Bermuda, you must apply glyphosate in the spring or summer, rather than during the winter months, when it is dormant. Water the lawn well to promote growth, then apply the herbicide, being sure to follow the instructions. A few weeks later, after the lawn has turned brown, water it again to get any viable stems and roots growing, at which point you can hit 'em again with the herbicide. A third application should pretty much ensure eradication. Since your yard does not exist in a vacuum, weeds will return, brought in by birds, lawn mowers, and the wind, so even if you use herbicides to remove your lawn, you will still have to be vigilant about controlling weeds, although generally to a much lesser degree.

NEGLECT

It is amazing that we have any lawns at all in much of California; it is hot and dry most of the year, and in some places eight consecutive months can pass without appreciable rain. Still, here we are discussing how best to rid our yards of this entrenched enemy. Why not just take it off life support? Stop watering, fertilizing, and preventing diseases, and see what happens?

As obvious as this may sound, it works...with a few caveats. (It wouldn't be gardening without the caveats!) Bermuda, kikiyou, and even St. Augustine grasses are used in California because they are fairly drought tolerant, so getting rid of them is a little harder than just cutting off the water supply. Although Bermuda grass requires some assistance to form the dense green lawn we prefer, it is a noxious weed that grows well in many untended, disturbed areas, so it will not just disappear on its own.

In my side yard, beneath a large deodar cedar, there is a small garden that was once covered with a struggling lawn, mostly St. Augustine. One day I just stopped watering the lawn, and several months later I covered it with oak leaves to smother the remaining grass. My approach—neglect with a little suffocation—worked well, and weeds now rarely bother the beds and paths in this small garden.

Will simple neglect work in sunny gardens? A gardener friend of mine did just this in his light-filled yard with great success. No backache, no chemicals, no yard waste, no disturbance, and now, several years later, no lawn.

So what are the disadvantages? The big one is that this method will not work in sunny gardens with weedy Bermuda or kikiyou grass unless you are vigilant about removing weeds as they appear. In fact, you will have to be so vigilant that we may want to list this method under mechanical removal. Sunny areas that receive regular water through irrigation or rain will most likely require significant weed control far into the future, so if that describes your space, one of the other methods mentioned in this chapter might be more effective at eradicating your yard of lawn and weeds. This method does, however, work well in shade (including beneath mature trees) and in hot, dry gardens that are not infested with intractable weeds like Bermuda grass or kikiyou.

LAWN REMOVAL METHODS PROS AND CONS

Method	Pros	Cons
Mechanical removal	• Can do anytime and can garden immediately after removal • Can be done gradually • Inexpensive • Chemical-free	• Causes soil disturbance that favors weeds • Requires extensive follow-up weed removal, especially with Bermuda grass • Labor-intensive • Causes the loss of some topsoil • Requires the disposal of weedy green waste
Suffocation by mulch	• Creates organic soil good for woodland and riparian plants • Can enrich nutrient-poor, sandy soils • Can make use of biodegradable yard waste • Mulch covering gives a finished, neat look • Chemical-free	• Organic-rich soil is not ideal for desert, chaparral, or scrub plants and may exacerbate future weed problems • Labor-intensive • Requires material for sheets and mulch • Mulch may slide or blow off paper surfaces
Solarization	• Heat kills microbials near the surface, some of which are disease-causing • Chemical-free	• Plastic can be expensive • Takes four to eight weeks and must be done in summer • Labor-intensive • Heat kills microbials near the surface, some of which are beneficial

Table continued on the next page.

LAWN REMOVAL METHODS
PROS AND CONS *continued*

Method	Pros	Cons
Solarization *continued*		• Heat may damage surface roots of nearby trees and shrubs • Not effective on certain seeds with hard shells (many weeds in the legume family) and some buried propagules (Bermuda grass stems)
Poison	• Easy to apply	• Expensive • Environmental and health risks associated with chemicals • Must be applied while plants are actively growing • May need to be repeated several times
Neglect	• Requires little effort • Most effective in dry, shady, or treed areas • Does not disturb the soil • No cost • Chemical-free	• Takes a long time, possibly months • May require follow-up weed removal • May not work in moist or wet areas • May not work for Bermuda grass in sunny areas

GARDEN INTERLUDE:
A SHARP INSTRUMENT AND A DREAM

G radually, as summer turns to fall, plans for my sidewalk garden emerge. The timing is good, since it is best to plant a California native garden in late fall to winter, when cooler temperatures and rainfall help plants adapt to their new homes. The garden will be wild, but not random or unplanned. I will plant the shrubs, grasses, and California sage scrub perennials in a repeating pattern to provide interest and order in the long, narrow strip. Although the garden will mimic drought-tolerant sage scrub habitat, young oak trees will be planted in the parkway, and over time the scrub will transition to woodland.

Late summer and autumn are brutal months in Southern California. It is dry—really dry. There has been no rain for nearly half a year. "June

Weedy grass used to cover my parkway from end to end.

My garden conversion began with lawn removal and planting in this
small patch in the parkway.

gloom," the period of cloudy, foggy weather common in early summer,
is but a memory. Each day starts off cool but mockingly sunny. By late
morning, it is *hot*.

Mornings are filled with the slow digging out of the weedy grass in
the parkway. Using a sharp spade, I outline a square and then shove the
blade under an edge, cutting and dislodging the tenacious roots. I remove
and shake out each square to leave as much topsoil but hopefully as few
stems and roots of Bermuda grass as possible. It is tedious, sweaty work
during which I get to meet and chat with neighbors who stroll by on this
busy street. Progress is slow.

The full length of the parkway is overwhelming and I am impatient.
I decide to break the project into smaller bits, starting with an eight-by-
six-foot rectangle at the north end of the strip. This way I will be able to
do what I am itching to do: plant something. The backbreaking process of
removing the grass will be divided into manageable pieces. After all, the
best way to start something big is to just dig in.

CHOOSE YOUR PLANTS

Now that you've cleared the way for a garden and have an idea of what plants might do well in your yard, it's time to acquire them by heading to a plant nursery! As I mentioned earlier, nurseries that specialize in California-friendly and native plants are more likely to have a good selection, but you may want to call ahead to check on availability. (For a list of native plant nurseries in Southern California, see Appendix D, starting on page 199.)

When I assist people at plant sales and nurseries, I am often asked to help them pick the best plant of the bunch, and in doing so I run through my mental list of desirable qualities. Of course, the most obvious things to check for are that the plant is pest-free and has healthy, green leaves, a healthy stem, and healthy roots. In short, it should look healthy.

Native plants, however, often look different from the common garden-center varieties. Not bred for sale, these plants sometimes seem—how shall I say it?— puny in comparison. They do best in the ground rather than in pots on a shelf. They thrive in our hot, dry climate using strategies that were not devised to withstand the kind of neglect or poor care they might suffer in the garden department of a big-box hardware store.

A poorly chosen plant—one that does not last, that brings disease and pests to your garden, or that never thrives to its potential—is not only a disappointment but also a waste of money. It is already hard to wait for a garden to fill in, and it's even worse when you end up with plants that struggle to stay alive. The good news is that as you gain experience with native plants, you will find that through better selection, planting, and care you will have more and more success, so don't be discouraged if you lose some in the beginning. The following tips are based on years of looking, growing, and learning, and hopefully they will save you from making some of the mistakes I made early on.

HOW TO SELECT NURSERY PLANTS

- Look for clean, healthy leaves
- Examine the stem
- Check the roots
- Don't bring home pests
- Select plants that are not too big, not too small
- Buy young
- Look for flowers in bud, not in bloom
- Know that a plant may be dormant, not dead

LOOK FOR CLEAN, HEALTHY LEAVES

The first thing most people do is look at a plant's leaves, and that's the perfect place to start. Minor damage is not a big concern, but browned tips or yellowing of leaves can indicate an accumulation of salts in the potting mix, whether from overfertilizing, disease, or a nutrient imbalance. Some native plants are deciduous, dropping their leaves seasonally or in response to drought, heat, or frost, and they may look unhealthy when in fact they are fine. Ask a staff person or consult a trusted source if you are not sure.

If you spy lots of new young leaves and few older leaves, this may indicate the plant is recovering from an earlier problem, like drought stress, pests, or a nutrient imbalance. If the problem is successfully treated, the plant will leaf out again and be fine; just be aware that somewhere along the line the plant may have been stressed and you might want to look for one that hasn't.

The woody stems of this wild sage indicate that it has been in its pot too long. It is better to choose a younger plant.

EXAMINE THE STEM

Check the stem for damage and breakage. For smaller pot sizes (up to one gallon), avoid plants that have thick, woody stems, since this can mean that the plant has been in its pot for too long.

The crown of a plant—where the stem goes up and the roots go down—is a very delicate area. Many diseases enter plants at this sensitive spot, so make sure it is undamaged and clean. The crown should be at or slightly above the soil level. When a plant is left in its pot too long, the potting mix sometimes washes out of the pot, or organic matter in the mix decomposes, both of which cause the plant to sink down. Unscrupulous nursery workers may then just "refurbish" the pot with a scoop of new soil, covering the crown. This is very bad! Not only is the plant growing in old, tired soil, but the buried crown is now more susceptible to disease. It is not always easy to see whether the crown is buried, but you can gently push the soil to the side to expose the surface roots or ask the nursery staff to check around the crown for you to make sure it is at the correct height.

CHECK THE ROOTS

It is critical to check the roots, but, alas, they are carefully hidden within the pot. So here is what you do: If the plant looks healthy from the soil up, lift the pot and check to see whether roots are coming out the bottom. A few tiny root hairs are probably no problem, but avoid plants

The roots of this hummingbird sage nicely fill the pot without being too crowded.

This wire grass is severely pot-bound (right). Usually grasses and other plants with fibrous roots do okay, even when pot-bound. It is helpful to tease the roots apart before planting (left).

with larger roots coming out the bottom, or those that show roots having been cut at the base of the container. To see whether the roots are packed against the pot wall, get a look inside by very carefully and gently squeezing the pot, or, better yet, ask the nursery staff for help. It would be best if you could pop the plant out of its container and thoroughly inspect the roots, but this may be frowned upon, since, like squeezing fruit at the market, it can damage good plants if done clumsily, so ask for help. Finally, pick up the pot and give it a good sniff. A sour or unpleasant smell indicates rotting in the root area. If you get one of these, put it down and walk away.

The significance of crowded roots varies depending on the degree of the problem and the type of plant. Grasses or other plants with fibrous roots usually do fine even if their roots are thick and matted. Plants with woody roots, however, can be very seriously impacted and should be avoided. Trees especially should be checked for this because the damage to the root structure may eventually kill the tree if not corrected. When a tree is allowed to remain in its container too long, its roots will circle the pot, and even if the plant is later transferred into a larger pot, the circling roots will not straighten out on their own. After the plant is placed in the garden, its circled roots will continue to grow in that pattern and eventually choke off water and nutrient flow to the rest of the tree. If the circling is not too extreme, the roots can be pruned and gently straightened, but it is nevertheless wise to always inspect roots of trees especially carefully before planting.

DON'T BRING HOME PESTS

Do not invite someone else's problems into your garden. Check beneath leaves and around the leaf stems and other tight little spots for pests. After accidentally bringing home plants with mealybugs, I've tried to fix the issue by carefully washing the leaves and dabbing them with alcohol, but usually the mealybugs win out and I end up tossing the whole mess. Better to leave the bugs at the nursery in the first place.

Check for aphids and scale on stems and on and under leaves. Slugs and snails may be lurking under dead leaves on the surface of the potting medium. Also, run your finger under the pot and in the drainage holes to check for these slimy pests. If you find several of them on or around the pot, it is best to leave those plants behind since the soil may contain their eggs as well.

SELECT PLANTS THAT ARE NOT TOO BIG, NOT TOO SMALL

Choosing a properly sized plant does not mean picking the largest one in the group. We all like to get the most for our money, but an oversize plant may indicate that it has been in its pot too long, meaning its roots may be crowded and it is more likely to be generally stressed and prone to transplant shock.

On the other end of the spectrum, the smallest plant in the group is either the youngest or it is stunted for some reason. I don't worry much about it being the youngest (although who wants to pay for a one-gallon pot when the plant is really a four-incher in oversize clothes?), but small size could also be an indicator of poor growth due to insufficient water, crowding by faster-growing neighbors, or a genetic weakness. Whatever the cause—and in most cases you will never know—the important thing is to pick a plant that is neither too big nor too small for its pot.

It is not always easy to tell exactly what the correct plant size is for a given container, but taking a look at the roots and stem, as described above, can give you some clues. Keep in mind that native plants in nursery pots may look scrawny when compared with commercial ornamentals that have been bred to look good on a nursery shelf.

BUY YOUNG

The longer a plant resides in a nursery, the more chance there is for plant stress. Most varieties transplant best when young, meaning they experience less transplant shock and often quickly catch up with older, larger plants. Furthermore, younger plants in smaller pots are easier to manage and they're less expensive to start with. For this reason, I rarely buy plants in pots larger than one gallon.

LOOK FOR FLOWERS IN BUD, NOT IN BLOOM

Nurseries know that flowers sell plants, but you know better. Select the plants that are in bud (often hidden under the table) so that you, rather than the nursery, get to enjoy the full flowering period.

Nurseries use flowers to facilitate the impulse buy. Be wiser and select the plants below that are in bud.

KNOW THAT A PLANT MAY BE DORMANT, NOT DEAD

Some plants, including syca-mores, redbuds, alders, and buckeyes, exhibit a period of dormancy, even in nursery con-tainers. While entering into dor-mancy the leaves may curl or look generally unhealthy. Do

Dormant desert peaches.

not let senescent (aging) leaves or leafless branches scare you off; small buds on the branches indicate that it is alive and well, just sleeping.

One of the first native plants I bought, way back in 2001, was a desert four-o'clock. At Rancho Santa Ana Botanic Garden's fall plant sale, a member of the nursery staff handed me a one-gallon container filled with what looked to be nothing more than potting soil, inform-ing me that it was a great plant. It was high priced for a one-gallon, and as far as I could tell there wasn't much there. Intrigued, I bought it anyway. When I got home and showed it to my husband, I felt like Jack of beanstalk fame, squandering the family fortune for a handful of nothing. Fifteen years later, this plant grows each spring, bursts into bloom each June, and then dies back to nothing each fall. I bend down and in one motion lift the tangle of dormant stems—which just detach from the roots—and throw it into the compost pile, awaiting the plant's return the next spring. The moral of the story is shop at nurseries with knowledgeable staff and high-quality merchandise.

Desert four-o'clock in full bloom.

This desert four-o'clock is dormant but will resprout in the spring.

GARDEN INTERLUDE:
PLANT SALE!

I enter a local chain store holding my plant list and a couple of gardening books. Although it is late fall and few native plants are in bloom, the nursery is bursting with color. Here in SoCal, many nonnative garden plants will flower all year in our mild climate as long as they get watered.

The bright colors are enticing, but I stay focused. My garden of natives will have plants that thrive in our climate because they have evolved in it, not because they have been bred to it. Most will bloom in spring when the soils are moist and just starting to warm up after the chilly winter. They have the good sense to slow down when it is hot and dry, and few look like much in the late fall, after the long summer drought.

I scan the area but cannot seem to find the natives, even though the nursery advertises having California native and "California friendly" plants. A pleasant sales employee tells me that they do, indeed, have natives. He shows me rosemary, lavender, and santolina. Though I am new to this, I know that these are not California natives. Low-water-use and possibly California friendly, sure, but these three plants come from the Mediterranean region of Europe. After I suggest that these are not actually native, the salesman responds, "Well, they are native somewhere." I cannot dispute that!

Finally we arrive at the actual California native section. It is a very small area with about fifteen different types of plants. Unlike most of the other specimens in the nursery, not a single one is in bloom. In fact, they all look rather puny. Still, I am excited to see a couple of sages, a toyon, some ceanothus, and manzanita. I go home with one native sage.

My next shopping adventure is quite different. Rather than going to a "regular" nursery, this time I go to a nursery that sells only native plants. Cozier and more natural looking, the plants in this nursery are displayed outdoors and on the ground. Few are in bloom, but the sheer number of options is enough to get me excited, although I am suddenly as nervous as I am happy. Signs in front of groups of plants provide information on

their types, sizes, and preferred growing conditions. The number of different species and cultivars—particularly since all are identified with long,
complicated botanical names—is overwhelming. Even worse, among this
mind-numbing assortment I can't find some of the plants I had selected
before coming, and I see many plants I know nothing about.

Consulting my list and my book, I become increasingly confused.
Finally I give up and just start walking through the rows of plants. A sales-
person asks if I need help, but I decline, preferring to muddle through
this new world alone. Refusing to allow myself to become intimidated
into inaction, I decide to just "buy it and try it." I select a few sages and
bunchgrasses and a ceanothus, and I go home happy.

As it turns out, some of these "unplanned" plants work out better than
I could have hoped. The ceanothus grows rapidly and is a showstopper
with its clusters of deep-blue flowers. Some of the sages fare very well, and
others less so. Over time I am beginning to know which plants do best in
my garden, but there are so many to choose from that there is still room
for pleasant surprises.

The annual autumn plant sale of my local chapter of the
California Native Plant Society.

PLANTING ADVICE

A few years ago a wonderful group of students from a local college teamed up with some Girl Scouts and spent the Martin Luther King Jr. National Day of Service planting new plants in the South Pasadena– Arroyo Seco Woodland and Wildlife Park. To begin the day I gave a quick demonstration on how to put plants in the ground. I was worried they would think I was being condescending, since I was basically telling them, "You just dig a hole and stick it in."

Well, I learned a lot that day. There are many things I take for granted when I garden—little "tricks" that are now second nature to me, since I have seen what happens when I don't do them. It turns out there's more to planting than just plopping a plant in a hole.

One of the most important tricks is to make absolutely sure that I do not place plants too close together. This is harder than it sounds when you are putting in a plant that will more than quadruple its size in just a few years. When I plant, I keep in mind the size of the full-grown plant and then I use a tape measure to check the spacing.

Another thing that I have learned from observing new plants is that, without careful planting, air pockets can develop around the roots, and this can lead to the plants drying out quickly, which then means they need extra watering. If you push down on the root area around a plant that has been in the garden for a year or less, you may find that the highly organic soil from the original nursery pot has decomposed, leaving large air pockets around the roots. When planting, I always check the potting soil, and if it has a lot of organic matter, I gently shake off as much as possible before placing the plant in the hole. I then gently but firmly pat the root area to remove air pockets, while being careful not to compact the soil too much. Even with this precaution I follow up by checking the root area for air pockets for several months.

That's just one example of a trick I've picked up from years of experience. Here are a few more I have learned about how to stick a plant in the dirt.

HOW TO PLANT NATIVE PLANTS

1. Check the weather forecast
2. Plant in moist soil
3. Hydrate before transplanting
4. Dig a hole
5. Decant the plant
6. Set the plant in the hole
7. Fill in the hole
8. Create a berm
9. Spread the mulch
10. Water thoroughly
11. Help mature plants make way

1. CHECK THE WEATHER FORECAST

Even during fall and winter, when temperatures are generally more moderate and rain more likely, we can experience weather conditions not ideal for planting. Do not plant if Santa Ana winds or extremely high temperatures are in the forecast.

2. PLANT IN MOIST SOIL

It is best not to plant when soil is saturated, since working in very wet soil can lead to compaction. Allow time for soil to partially dry following heavy or long periods of rain. If the soil is dry, water a day before planting so soil is moderately and evenly moist.

3. HYDRATE BEFORE TRANSPLANTING

Make sure that the container plant is well hydrated before you transplant it. Water it well several hours before transplanting.

Gently remove the plant from its pot and loosen its roots.

4. DIG A HOLE

The hole should be as deep as but wider than the root ball. If you are planting in clay soil, dig a hole at least twice as wide as the root ball and use a hand rake to roughen the sides of the hole. Some gardeners fill the planting hole with water and allow it to drain before planting. As noted above, the hole and the surrounding soil should be moist before the plant is put in.

5. DECANT THE PLANT

Leave the plant in the pot until the moment before you are going to plant it. Decanting it too early can stress a plant, since its roots can become dried and damaged when left out in the open. Unless you are working with a plant that has brittle or delicate roots, gently shake off some of the potting soil and then tease apart the outer roots. If the roots are circling the pot, unwind them and stretch them out. If the plant is extremely pot-bound and has a fibrous root system, like grasses, you can be quite brutal, cutting, tearing, and teasing the matted roots apart. (For more information, see "How to Select Nursery Plants," starting on page 128.)

6. SET THE PLANT IN THE HOLE

When you place the plant in the hole, make sure that the root crown (the spot where the stems go up and the roots go down) is level with the surface or slightly above it. Adjust the size of the hole as needed.

7. FILL IN THE HOLE

Use surrounding soil to fill the hole. Do not add amendments or fertilizers. Many native plants are adapted to California's mostly lean soil, and giving them extra nutrients in this way often forces excessive growth that the plant cannot support. The soft green leaves and stems of plants that grow too rapidly are also more susceptible to pests, diseases, and dehydration. They often don't make it through the long, hot summer drought.

Contrary to what you might think, adding amendments to the planting hole in "problematic" soil can exacerbate existing issues. Filling a planting hole in clay soil with a well-drained mix makes it more difficult for the roots of the young plant to break out of the hole and extend into the native soil. Furthermore, as water fills the planting hole that contains the well-drained soil, it cannot easily soak into the surrounding clay, and so the roots end up sitting in water and rotting. On the other end of the scale, amendments added to lean, well-drained soil can decompose or wash out very quickly, and though they may not cause any great problems, they usually do not help much either, so you might as well save your money. If you feel that you must add amendments to poor soil, mix it with the surrounding soil, gradually decreasing the amount of new soil as you move away from the plant. (For tips on working with lean and heavy soils, see pages 33 to 37.)

With your plant in the hole and tucked in, pat down the soil. Be gentle but firm. Eliminate air pockets, but do not overly compact the soil. It takes a bit of experience, but most people are too gentle. Don't stomp on the ground, but don't use too light a touch either.

8. CREATE A BERM

Create a raised ring of soil a little beyond the edge of the planting hole to keep the water from running off. You may need to remove the berm later if the plant gets waterlogged from excessive rain or irrigation.

MULCH

Mulch is a top-dressing for soil. There are two main types: organic and inorganic. Organic mulch includes woodchips, bark, and partially decomposed compost, while inorganic mulch can be rocks, pebbles, decomposed granite, or even shredded tires.

Organic mulch looks good and works well in this woodland garden at the Prisk Schoolyard Habitat Garden in Long Beach.

Benefits:

- Moderates soil temperature
- Conserves water
- Controls weeds
- Reduces erosion
- Improves soil structure
- Looks good

How to choose it:

- Follow Mother Nature. Organic mulch keeps the soil moist and, in time, enriches the soil, so it is best used for woodland and riparian plants adapted to those conditions. Inorganic mulch is best for gardens that feature desert, chaparral, or scrub plants—dry-adapted varieties that thrive in well-drained, nutrient-poor soil.

- Do not use rubber or shredded tire mulch. Although it does not decompose and therefore won't have to be replaced, it is not as effective in controlling weeds, it is highly flammable and difficult to extinguish once it begins burning, and it contains a number of metal and organic contaminants with known environmental and/or human health risks.

- Use clean mulch. Avoid material that may contain weed seeds, pesticides, or other toxins. Use green waste from your own property to reduce the amount of waste you generate.

How to use it:

- Maintain a four-to-six-inch-thick layer of mulch—thick enough to suppress weeds, but not so thick as to hinder air and water circulation. Replenish organic mulch as it decomposes.
- Keep mulch away from trunks or stems of plants.
- Leave some ground free of mulch, since many native solitary bees nest in bare soil. Mulch-free, undisturbed soil provides habitat for these important pollinators.

Decomposed granite mulch is appropriate for this dryland garden.

Keep mulch away from the stem of the plant.

9. SPREAD THE MULCH

Your mulch layer should be about four to six inches deep, and you should keep it clear of the plant stems.

10. WATER THOROUGHLY

Water the new planting once, then go drink a beer. Come back and water again, checking that the root area and the surrounding soil is thoroughly wet. This process seems easy, but it can be surprisingly difficult, especially in heavy and clay-rich soils. You might even need to go out a third time about an hour later to water once more. Once the plant area has been well soaked, do not water the plant again until the soil has started to dry out. Depending on the soil type and weather conditions, you may not need to water again for a week or two. To check the soil moisture, dig down a few inches with a hand trowel or a soil probe. You don't want to overwater, but it is just as important that the soil does not get too dry before you water again. You do not want to stress these tender plants.

11. HELP MATURE PLANTS MAKE WAY

A fellow plantsman passed along another little tip for planting near mature shrubs and trees. Since these older plants have extensive root systems, chances are high that they will quickly send their roots into the soft, moist soil of the hole you have dug for the new plant. To give the youngster a chance to compete, use a spade to cut the roots of the mature plant in a circle around the new plant. Insert the spade about eight inches down around the new plant, making sure to do it beyond the root ball. Repeat this several times during the first year or two, until the new plant has had a chance to send its roots into the surrounding soil and is on its own.

GARDEN INTERLUDE:
PLANTING TIME

F inally, after all the hard work of planning, preparing, and acquiring plants, it is time to plant my garden! Plan in hand, I retrieve my tape measure, spade, and the one-gallon plants that I recently purchased.

A couple of days ago, in preparation for this glorious moment, I watered the strip. The soil had been quite dry, so it took a long time with a very gentle spray to moisten the soil down to about ten inches. In fact, I had to water it several times to allow the water to penetrate the soil to the desired depth. It can be surprisingly difficult to moisten dry soil, but now it is neither too wet nor too dry, and the moist soil has a rich, earthy smell. I garden for many reasons, and the smell of healthy soil is not the least of them.

Next, I place the pots approximately where they are shown on my plan, making slight corrections based on how they look in real life. I measure the

Place plants according to plan, making adjustments as necessary.

distance between plants with my tape measure to ensure I do not place the plants too close together or too close to the sidewalk. Although the plants are very small now, I know that they will get to be the size indicated on their labels. The deer grass alone will grow to three feet wide. Suddenly I notice that the label on the Frosty Blue California lilac says that it grows to nine feet in height and width. I selected this plant because, unlike some other California lilacs, it does well in garden conditions, but I missed the part about nine feet. The parkway is only six feet wide! Too late now. I go ahead and plant it because I have no other place to put it, and in my naivety, I figure that it can't really get that big, and anyway, I can always prune it. (Note: Five years later this proved to be a mistake!)

My spade bites easily into the loamy soil. The hole is only as deep as the distance from the crown to the bottom of the root ball, and following advice about planting natives, I do not add amendments or fertilizers. Gently I ease the first plant out of its pot. Although it is small, its roots look good, neither too dense nor too light. I carefully loosen them and place the plant in the hole, making sure the crown is slightly higher than the level of the surrounding soil. Next, I gently but firmly pack the soil

Create berms around each plant, then carefully water to make sure that the entire root area is thoroughly moistened.

Lightly sprinkle organic matter in the planted bed.

from the hole back around the plant, pushing soil into any air pockets I find with my fingers. Finally, I create a small berm about twelve inches in diameter around the plant to direct the water to the roots rather than allowing it to run off.

I repeat this for the rest of the plants, putting them in the ground, stepping back to look, and then replanting one or two in slightly different places as I try to visualize them when they have filled in. After all of the buildup, the planting is almost anticlimactic, but it sure is fun.

Once everything is in the ground, I get some partially decomposed leaves from my compost pile and spread them over the entire bed, leaving room around each plant so the stems stay clear and dry. The process is completed with a thorough soaking for each and every new plant.

It looks nice but kind of empty. I hope the plants get as big as they say!

As I start sweeping the sidewalk and putting things away, I notice my neighbor looking over my work. This is the same one who had informed me of a city ordinance regulating what is planted in the parkway. I make a mental note to see whether I can find out about the ordinance without actually asking a city employee.

Annual wildflowers fill in my young parkway garden.

MUST A NEW GARDEN LOOK SPARSE?

A new garden can seem a little bare. This may be a source of concern for you (and your neighbors), especially if you're ripping out an established garden or a manicured lawn. You may be thinking you can avoid this problem by placing the plants closer together and then removing some as they fill in. Or maybe you are considering buying older plants that start out bigger. I hate to break it to you, but neither approach is a good long-term solution. Instead, I encourage you to take an old-fashioned approach, one that requires an old-fashioned trait: patience. This can be hard to accept, especially during a time when teams of "professionals" on TV enter the lives of Jane and Joe Ordinary and in a few harrowing days convert home and yard into a designer's dream via "extreme makeover."

But there's little reality in reality television. In the world we live in, new plants are small, they take a while to get established, and so it takes time to fill the empty spaces of a young garden. Placing plants too close together is one of the most common errors new gardeners make, especially with native plants, but it's easily avoided with a little planning. Believe that the spindly twig in the one-gallon container will reach its predicted size—and often quicker than you expect. If you do not leave enough room, you will be faced with losses as some plants get crowded out. Even if they do not die, you will be compelled to prune back the overreaching behemoths as they burst out of their meagerly allocated spaces.

It would be lovely if you could just plant twice as much as needed and then remove some specimens once things start filling in. Yes, it would cost a bit more, but the garden would not look quite so skimpily clad in the beginning. The problem with this is that, as bad luck would have it, the plants you eventually want to remove for design reasons are usually the strongest, healthiest, and prettiest, while those sitting in exactly the right places are struggling, dying, or dead. Plants are living things, and they do not always perform the way we would like. So yes, overplanting might help with aesthetics early on, but in the long run it will probably create more problems than it solves.

The second "modern solution" to our desire for instant results is to start with larger, older plants. Why put in a tiny one-gallon when you could plant a five- or even a fifteen-gallon? For one thing, the more time spent in a nursery, the more abuse or neglect a plant may be subjected to. Often, the repeated stress from improper care and watering is not apparent while the plant is in the rich, sterile potting mix, but once you get it home to your garden, it may be more likely to fail in its new conditions.

Sometimes plants at nurseries are not moved into larger containers often enough and they become pot-bound, their roots circling the container rather than developing a good branching structure. (For more information, see "How to Select Nursery Plants," starting on page 128.) When they are repotted, they may do fine for a while, but their roots will never develop a strong, healthy structure, and they will be stunted and ailing, often failing within a year or two.

The best solution to filling in a sparse new garden is to plant short-lived perennials and annuals between the young plants. I often sow wildflower seeds, especially California poppies, to make my new beds look full and attractive. Monkeyflowers and penstemons are fast-growing, short-lived perennials that add color to a young garden. California poppies are great, but be aware that if you use an aggressive grower like that, you must be brutal and remove those that are crowding or growing over your long-term plants, which need room both above and below the ground to get a good start.

Adding annuals and fast-growing perennials is not only fun in and of itself, it also means the first spring of your new garden will be a riot of color, and your neighbors will spend only about five months of the year wondering whether you were too cheap or too poor to add more plants. The following steps will help you create a wildflower display in your new garden, while also serving to remind you to take time to go out in search of the fields of awe-inspiring spring wildflowers that grace our remarkable state.

HOW TO GROW WILDFLOWERS

1. Purchase seeds from a reputable source
2. Remove weeds and lightly roughen the surface of the soil
3. Sow seeds in late fall to winter
4. Create good seed-to-soil contact
5. Water gently
6. Control weeds
7. Additional tips

1. PURCHASE SEEDS FROM A REPUTABLE SOURCE

The first step to a beautiful wildflower garden is acquiring seeds. Many wildflower seed mixes include invasive nonnatives, so be sure to purchase seeds from reputable growers that specialize in California natives. (For a list of sources, see Appendix D, starting on page 199.) If possible, use locally native wildflower seeds, but note that it is illegal and unethical to harvest seeds from public lands without a permit. Wildflowers have been in decline for many years; leave the seeds in place.

As a rough guideline, a half-ounce of seed will cover approximately twenty-five square feet, although this can vary depending on seed size. Seed mixes prepared by reputable sources include annuals that are adapted to similar conditions, such as dry shade, coast, or mountain mixes.

2. REMOVE WEEDS AND LIGHTLY ROUGHEN THE SURFACE OF THE SOIL

Weeds are often a major impediment to a successful wildflower garden, so it is important to remove as many weeds as possible before seeding. If you have peeled back the lawn, then you have probably taken care of most of this, but look out for seeds and bits of stems that can grow new roots. Since it is easier to remove weeds from an empty bed than to try to work around wildflower seedlings and young plants, water newly exposed garden beds several weeks before seeding to encourage weed growth. It won't take long to clear the ground of these new unwanted sprouts.

Once you are ready to sow the seeds, lightly roughen the surface of the soil with a rake. Deep cultivating is unnecessary and counterproductive, since disturbing the soil brings up additional weed seed and makes it easier for weeds to grow. You can also sprinkle a light layer of coarse gravel in the wildflower bed. Both methods—raking lightly and spreading coarse gravel—are intended to provide nooks and crannies so seeds have better contact with the soil, which keeps them from drying out.

This wildflower bed is marked with chalk to help gardeners distribute wildflower seeds at Rancho Santa Ana Botanic Garden.

3. SOW SEEDS IN LATE FALL TO WINTER

It is best to sow seeds before or during the rainy season, from late fall to winter, preferably right before rain is predicted. Continue sowing over a period of weeks to extend the period of bloom. In milder regions, and with certain plants like the California poppy, it is okay to continue seeding into spring.

Seeds can be sown in mixes of several types of compatible seeds or in drifts of single types. Large, coarse seeds, like poppies, are easy to sow by hand. Fine seeds, like tansy-leafed phacelia, can be "bulked up" with sand or sawdust for more even distribution, and a kitchen-spice or powdered-sugar shaker can also be used to scatter seeds. Another technique suggested by a colleague at Rancho Santa Ana is to toss the seeds gently into the air with one hand while batting at the seeds with the other. This fast and effective technique is useful for large areas.

Gardeners sow seeds in drifts within marked areas.

4. CREATE GOOD SEED-TO-SOIL CONTACT

As mentioned above, it is important for the seeds to have good contact with the soil. If they are lying lightly on top of the soil, they will dry out, blow away, or be eaten by birds. After sowing, rake the surface very gently, and consider adding a light layer of either fine, weed-free organics or gravel to keep the seeds from drying out. Avoid using large wood chips, since the big chunks block sunlight and smother the new seeds, while also providing an excellent hiding place for slugs and snails that truly appreciate a gourmet spread of wild seed sprouts.

5. WATER GENTLY

Water with a fine spray to moisten soil and seeds, and to improve seed-soil contact. If rain is sparse, water gently to keep beds moist as the seeds germinate and begin to grow. For many native wildflowers, you

Volunteers carefully remove nonnative weeds growing among new wildflower seedlings.

can taper off supplemental water when the annuals are a few inches tall during winters with average rainfall. Provide supplemental water in dry winters and in spring to extend the bloom period.

6. CONTROL WEEDS

It is essential to stay on top of weeds to prevent them from quickly overwhelming the new wildflowers. When you start the garden, sow some wildflower seeds in pots so you can learn how to differentiate wildflower seedlings from weed seedlings. If weeds or insects are decimating the seedlings, you can transplant the wildflowers that were grown in pots once they are large enough (about four inches tall) to make it in the cruel world of the garden.

7. ADDITIONAL TIPS

• Remove wildflowers (and weeds) that are crowding new perennial plantings. Show no mercy.

I sowed these wildflower seeds in containers to help me distinguish weeds from wildflowers in the garden. The containers full of wildflowers look lovely in spring as well.

Baby blue eyes growing in a container.

Leave some wildflower seeds for the birds.

Wildflower seeds that I collected from my parkway garden in late summer.

A wildflower display at Rancho Santa Ana Botanic Garden, with farewell-to-spring, yellow lupine, and grand linanthus.

- Cut flowers for bouquets, and "deadhead" (i.e., remove spent flowers) to extend the bloom period.

- Collect seeds in late spring to summer for next year's garden, but leave some for the birds. Store seeds in a cool, dry place.

- Most residential gardens will look better if you remove spent annuals at the end of the season, although from a habitat standpoint it is best not to rush this. Balance between keeping your neighbors happy and providing for the birds.

- If you want wildflowers to reseed during the following spring, do not water during summer, since the seeds will rot in hot, wet soil.

GARDEN INTERLUDE:
STINGY

While taking a horticulture class at a local community college, my professor made a joke one day about his neighbor's newly installed native plant garden. The proud neighbor had called my teacher over to show off his new landscape, and my teacher, who has an outstanding ability to instruct and entertain at the same time, joked in his good-natured way that his neighbor was either cheap or short of funds because he had used so few plants. We all got the joke because it was understood in our class that native plants start out small and need to be well spaced to create a successful garden. Looking now at my new sidewalk garden, I was sure

My parkway garden planted in October 2002.

Poppies and other wildflowers emerge in March 2003.

that my teacher would get a chuckle out of it, but I was also sure that I would have the last laugh!

Still, I wanted my garden to make a good impression in my conventional-looking neighborhood. I wanted people to see the beauty of these plants from the start. The solution is easy: wildflowers. To create a truly spectacular display in spring, I would sprinkle wildflower seeds in this new garden bed in late fall.

I had already spread mulch between the infant plants, and I wondered whether I could just sprinkle the seeds on top. Experienced native gardeners informed me that this would not work, since the seeds would probably rot in the mulch, and those that managed to germinate would have difficulty setting their roots into soil. Following this advice, I raked the mulch away, roughed the soil surface, sprinkled the seeds, and applied a thin layer of mulch on top. Next I watered the area with a soft, shower-like spray.

By April 2003, wildflowers fill the bed.

The wildflower seeds were easy-to-grow annuals, including California poppies, tidy-tips, bird's-eye gilia, globe gilia, and tansy-leafed phacelia. (For a list of annual wildflowers I have grown in my garden, see Appendix B, starting on page 194.) A few months later, the garden was full to bursting with color and pollinators. Family and neighbors could not help but notice the beauty of this new native garden.

KEEP YOUR GARDEN ALIVE

CONGRATULATIONS ON YOUR new garden! I hope that now that the hard work is done, you are taking time to enjoy the space you created. However, there are a few more things that you need to know to give your plants the best chance for success during the critical establishment period. This is the time during which the plant becomes rooted in and acclimated to its new home. This section provides information on what the establishment period is, how long it lasts, and what you can do to help your plants adapt to and thrive in their new location.

HELP YOUR PLANTS BECOME ESTABLISHED

Transitioning from nursery conditions that promote fast, soft growth to the harsh, cruel world of your garden can be difficult. You need to pamper your new plants through this adjustment period, but you may be wondering how long you will have to do this and how you will know when they are established.

Plants—like people—vary in how quickly they become established in a new place. As a general rule, trees take longer than shrubs, which take longer than herbaceous perennials, but there is also variation within the forms. The California lilac shrub, for example, grows and establishes fairly rapidly, while toyon, another native shrub, takes much longer to get going. A rule of thumb is that it takes one to three growing seasons for plants to become established, and generally they triple in size during that time.

There are some aboveground hints that let you know a plant is becoming established. When the roots of a newly planted perennial

Frosty Blue California lilac planted in October 2002 from a one-gallon pot.

Frosty Blue California lilac three years in the ground, approximately five feet tall and wide.

start to penetrate the surrounding soil, the plant often requires less frequent watering and is less likely to wilt on a hot day. It may also start to grow faster. In general, it seems tougher than it did before. Following are some important gardening tips to help your delicate new plantings acclimate to your garden. Most have to do with proper watering, although I have also included a few other tricks to protecting your new specimens.

WATERING WISDOM

One of the most common questions new gardeners ask is how often and for how long new plants should be watered. Unfortunately, there is no simple answer to this question; there are just too many variables. How old are the plants? What type of soil are they in? Does the garden get a lot of wind? Is it sunny or shady? Is it a coastal garden or is it inland? Weather conditions also affect water needs, and they are not static. Has it recently been hot and sunny or overcast and cool? Has there been any rain? Variations of all of these factors can affect how much water a plant requires.

In this section, I advocate that you water new plants according to their individual needs. If you have grouped together plants with similar water requirements, in time you will be able to water *areas* rather than individual plants. Furthermore, if you have selected plants that are well adapted to the climate, you should not need to water often after these plants become established. Until that time, here are some guidelines for watering young plants.

HOW AND WHEN TO WATER

- Water when needed
- Water thoroughly
- Check beneath the mulch
- Allow the soil to dry
- Water less often as plants become established
- Don't water wilted plants if the soil is wet
- Water like Mother Nature

WATER WHEN NEEDED

This first suggestion seems so obvious as to be ridiculous, but I must mention it because it is, in fact, the most important. Good gardeners do not follow rigid watering schedules but rather water when they notice the plants need it.

The curled, drooping leaves of this young monkeyflower suggest extreme drought stress. It is best to water before a plant reaches this condition.

As young plants usually need water more often than older, established plants, water when the soil near the roots and beneath the surface is dry. Check plants for early signs of drought stress, such as slight wilting of leaves or stem tips, but be aware that plants with stiff stems and waxy leaves may not wilt, even when they need water. If a lush plant exhibits signs of drought stress, assume that its more rigid neighbors need water too. It is best to water before plants become too stressed.

A good gardener also pays attention to the weather forecast. If hot, dry weather is predicted, water before it arrives. A plant whose stems, leaves, and roots are adequately hydrated is better equipped to withstand desiccating conditions, including strong winds. Hydrated plants also survive frost better than thirsty ones.

Continue to carefully monitor your plants during the first, second, and third growing seasons. Remember to provide supplemental water during dry winters for both young and established plants. This is the time that native plants, especially those from chaparral, grassland, and scrub areas, do most of their growing, so give them a little help. Without supplemental watering, even previously healthy, strong trees and shrubs may go into decline if there are several consecutive years of drought.

WATER THOROUGHLY

Make sure the soil in and around the plant's roots becomes thoroughly wet. This means that the soil both below and beyond the original planting hole should be moistened. If you only water the planting hole, water will be drawn from the hole into the dry soil surrounding it. The only way to know that you have watered deeply enough is to use a trowel or soil probe to check the soil a few inches down. When you do this, be careful not to damage roots by digging into them.

The type of soil you have will also determine how you water. Since water penetrates sandy soils quickly, the length of time you need to water it is usually fairly short, but you will need to irrigate more frequently because sandy soil also dries out quickly.

It can take extra time to properly water poorly drained, heavy soil. In order to thoroughly saturate this kind of soil, you may need to water for long intervals but very lightly, so the water can sink in instead of run off. If you still have a problem with water running off or pooling, try watering lightly for a short period and then waiting awhile before doing this again. This technique, referred to as *interval watering,* is slow and tedious, but if done correctly you should not need to water again for quite a while, since heavy soil also takes a long time to dry out. One final tip on watering heavy clay soil: it is best not to allow clay soil to dry out completely. When clay soil dries, it draws water from plant roots, becomes very hard, and can be quite difficult to moisten. Over time, as plants start to grow and worms and other animals work the soil, both heavy and lean soils will improve and be easier to water. Be patient!

CHECK BENEATH THE MULCH

Check the soil beneath the mulch to make sure it is wet. It is easy to moisten organic mulch without providing adequate water to the soil, so don't rely on surface moisture alone. The danger in having wet mulch but dry soil is that roots will grow into the mulch but not the surrounding soil. These shallow roots do not anchor the plant well; they desiccate quickly when the weather is hot and dry, and are more likely to rot when the mulch is warm and moist.

ALLOW THE SOIL TO DRY

Soil should be moderately dry before you water it again, since many native plants are susceptible to rot and disease if their roots stay too wet. This is especially important in clay soils, since plants can rot out in both warm, wet soils and in colder soils when there is little active growth. As mentioned earlier, however, do not allow clay soil to become overly dry.

WATER LESS OFTEN AS PLANTS BECOME ESTABLISHED

You can reduce watering frequency as plants become established, although when you do water, continue to do so until the root area and beyond is wet. Do not forget to water during dry winters.

DON'T WATER WILTED PLANTS IF THE SOIL IS WET

Plants wilt for many reasons. If wilting is due to root rot from excess water, it may look like the plant needs water when in fact additional irrigation will only make the problem worse. Plants with root rot are unlikely to recover, though it may help to gently prune back the tips of the stems and allow the soil to dry. Follow up with careful watering practices: only water when the soil is moderately dry and the plant looks like it needs a drink. Admittedly, this is a bit hard for novices to discern, but knowledge comes with practice.

WATER LIKE MOTHER NATURE

Well, not *exactly* like Mother Nature, since we are starting with nursery-grown plants that cannot survive the long summer drought

FACTORS THAT
AFFECT WATER NEEDS

Type of plant: Even among California native plants, water needs vary greatly. Western sycamores and alders, for example, grow along rivers and require year-round water. Coast live oaks grow on drier land and prefer dry summers. Know your plants and their specific watering preferences.

Age of plant: Young plants require extra water while adjusting to the change from nursery to garden conditions. Water young plants more often, reducing frequency as the plants mature.

Soil: Sandy soil saturates and dries more rapidly than heavier soils, so water it more often and for shorter periods. Watering sandy soil for long periods is wasteful because the water just passes through the soil below the root zone. With clayey soil, in contrast, water can take a while to penetrate to a proper depth, so you will need to water longer, but it also dries out more slowly, requiring less frequent irrigation.

Mulch: Mulch generally reduces water loss by slowing evaporation at the surface. Take care that water penetrates the soil beneath the mulch, and that mulch does not accumulate around the base of the plant.

Exposure: Both the amount of sun your plant receives and when it receives it impact water needs. Plants on the west side of buildings that receive late-afternoon sun will be hotter and drier than those on the east side bathed in morning sun but shaded in the afternoon. Observe your garden at different times of the day and year so you are familiar with exposure patterns.

Time of year: Seasonal variations in rainfall, sunlight, and temperature impact water needs, so adjust your watering schedule accordingly.

Climate: Although much of California has a Mediterranean climate, there are regional variations, including inland, coastal, foothill, high desert, and low desert areas. Climate also varies locally; some gardens near a beach may experience haze and fog while others not far away will bask in full sun most of the day. Pay attention to the conditions specific to your garden.

Microclimate: There are also climatic variations within a yard. For instance, lower areas can be sinks for cooler air, while areas in front of west-facing walls can experience extreme heat. Get to know your unique garden landscape.

Weather events: Young plants, and even some established plants, require extra irrigation during extreme weather events, such as Santa Ana winds or winter frost. Check your forecast, and water accordingly.

Neighboring plants: Plants growing under trees or surrounded by lawn will have to compete for water and nutrients. Since the garden is ever changing, the water needs of plants will need to be altered as they and their neighbors grow and change.

Irrigation: Irrigation efficiency influences how often and how much water is needed. In hot, windy conditions, or if sprinkler heads are poorly adjusted or broken, you can lose to evaporation half of your water from overhead irrigation. Water delivery—drip, overhead, rotor, or spray—is an important factor to consider when gauging how much to water.

Neighbor's irrigation: Runoff, drift, or underground flow of water from a neighbor's garden should be taken into account when you select plants and determine your watering practices.

before they have become established. You should, however, take a hint from Mother Nature by watering in winter when the rains fall short of average, especially during drought cycles.

During summer, water early in the morning when it is cooler and the winds are calm, or on those unusual cool, cloudy days. Fifty percent of overhead irrigation can be lost to evaporation in hot, windy conditions. Furthermore, pathogenic microorganisms are less active in cooler soils.

Although early morning is best, it is essential to monitor your irrigation system to prevent waste due to broken or misaligned sprinkler heads, so water late in the day if this is the only time you will see the irrigation system in action.

CODDLE THEM WHEN YOUNG

Although poor watering practices account for most plant losses, there are many other factors to consider when your plants are just starting out. The following suggestions will give your new plants a better chance of survival.

- Pat the soil
- Set up sun screens
- Remove weeds
- Manage pests
- Prune fast-growing shrubs
- Be patient

PAT THE SOIL

Every so often, especially if your young plant seems to need a lot of water, probe the soil with your fingers around the original root ball to determine whether large air pockets have developed. Organic matter in the nursery potting mix that surrounds the plant's roots decomposes over time, sometimes leaving gaps in the soil. Check plants often during the establishment period, particularly those that seem to go dry often.

SET UP SUN SCREENS

A temporary sun screen can help reduce stress on young plants that wilt during the heat of the day but perk up as temperatures drop. You

Sometimes young plants will wilt during the heat of the day—even if the soil is moist—because they are losing water from tender leaves more rapidly than they can replenish it. Screening these plants from direct sun can be helpful, but be sure to check the soil moisture frequently as well.

may only need it on especially hot days, so keep an eye on how your plant is doing in different weather and at different times of the day. In time, your plants will be better able to withstand heat and you can put away the shield.

REMOVE WEEDS

Dig out weeds that grow around new plants. These unwanted sprouts compete for water, nutrients, and light, and sometimes harbor insect pests and diseases. The same goes for wildflowers that crowd native perennials.

MANAGE PESTS

Aphids are common pests found on new plants. These tiny insects often appear with lush spring growth, and although the problem typically resolves itself during summer's heat, it is best to control aphids at once to alleviate plant stress. Prune and dispose of young aphid-infested stems, then carefully hose off heavily infested plants. The water stream should be hard enough to remove the insects without damaging the plant. Releasing lacewing larvae, which eat aphids, can help, and although ladybugs are often used for this purpose, their efficacy is debated. If you do use ladybugs, it is best to release the larvae rather than full-grown insects, since the youngsters have a large appetite and cannot fly away (to control pests in your neighbors' yards).

Ladybug larvae eat more than the familiar adult beetle and cannot fly away.

PRUNE FAST-GROWING SHRUBS

Fast-growing plants like monkeyflowers and many wild sages benefit from early pruning and tipping, or pinching back. This can improve the plant's mature shape and prevent breakage of long stems. Most other plants do not require or benefit from pruning for the first year or two. Young trees may also need pruning after this time to develop a good, strong structure.

BE PATIENT

Many native plants do not show much aboveground growth during the first year or two, but much is happening below the surface, where new root development is needed before the plant can increase in size. Do not worry if healthy-looking plants seem to be growing slowly—or not at all—during this time.

Observing your plants as they grow will teach you more about how to care for them than any book or class, and each "failure" is an opportunity to learn. If a plant dies, do a postmortem to try to determine what went wrong. Even if you cannot figure it out, you may want to try again. My rule is three strikes you're out: any plant that does not succeed in three tries is not meant to be in my garden. With so many wonderful native plants to choose from, look at this as an opportunity to try something new.

GARDEN INTERLUDE: LAZY GARDENING

One of my biggest goals is to hone my lazy-gardening skills, yet I know that my family laughs when I talk about how little time I spend in the garden. Yes, it is true that sometimes what seems to me to be a quick fifteen minutes in the garden turns out to be two hours by the clock. After all, I am a gardener, hence gardening is a passion, not a chore. Nevertheless, I recognize that not everyone shares my predilection for physical outdoor labor and dirt, and so I'd like to give a quick overview of the care required by my garden—with all its native and nonnative plants, mature trees, a small lawn, vegetables, container plants, and wildflowers—along with suggestions for reducing that amount of effort.

Unlike with traditional landscape gardening, I do not "mow and blow" each and every week of the year. Back when most of my yard was covered with lawn, we did engage a service for this task, which took two to three workers about thirty minutes per week to mow, blow, and edge the front yard. In addition to those four person-hours of labor per month, there was the noise, air pollution, and use of fuel that goes with this kind of work. As the years passed, my needs changed, particularly since the amount of

Grooming deer grass with a landscape rake in mid-spring involves combing out the dead blades.

lawn requiring constant maintenance shrunk to only a small patch of grass on the east side of the front yard and another bit in the back. One day, my gardener came to me and asked if we still needed his services. Since I was taking care of all of the non-lawn areas, the answer was obvious to both of us.

Mowing now is not much of an issue, and the remaining patches of grass look neat and healthy on a bimonthly or even less-frequent mowing schedule. I've replaced the large gasoline mowers with a cute small electric machine. Edging is still a challenge—it takes too long with my clippers, and I have not found another nonpolluting solution to my liking—but as the lawn continues to shrink, that problem will shrink with it.

As for watering, much of my yard, and especially the parkway and the back yard, consists of native plants that require little irrigation. However, my mature, nonnative trees (avocados, deodar, and citrus), the patches of lawn, the vegetable garden, several container plants, and any new plantings need careful, supplemental watering. Ridding the yard of these elements would reduce the workload, but I love my potted plants, garden tomatoes, and having a place for our young grandkids to toddle around, so the extra effort is worth it to me!

An automatic, low-volume irrigation system waters the vegetable garden. Each season the setup and removal takes some time, but once it is operating, the mini-sprinklers go off daily or every other day (depending on crop and weather), requiring only an occasional check to make sure everything is functioning properly. More importantly, this allows us to go on vacation without sacrificing our beloved tomatoes.

A traditional overhead sprinkler system irrigates the front lawn. When we travel I set it to go off once a week for about forty-five minutes per zone—long enough for the water to soak the soil to a depth of several inches. When we are home I monitor the front yard, setting the sprinkler to go off early in the morning whenever the lawn or shrubs show the slight wilting of leaves that suggests the beginnings of drought stress. I also follow the weather forecast and try to fully hydrate these nonnatives before the onset of extreme heat. The watering schedule is usually about once

The left half of my front lawn was removed—actually covered over—following a windstorm in late 2011. Debris from downed limbs was chipped and spread.

every ten days for the front yard, except during the winter, when we sometimes get enough rain to turn it off for much of the season.

The parkway oak trees, planted in 2005, have grown into adolescents. As expected—and hoped—the amount of work required by the parkway garden has diminished. The springtime wildflower display is less spectacular now that the trees and shrubs have spread, but the garden looks more settled. I do not water the parkway regularly, though I hand-water new plantings as needed.

As the garden has matured, there are fewer young plants each year, but, as in any living system, some plants die and new ones are added. As we have discussed throughout the book, these young plants require careful attention for the first few years, but once they become established they are relatively low-maintenance. A four-inch layer of mulch keeps the soil from getting too hot or drying out too quickly, and in my well-drained, loamy soil, even new plants generally require water only once a week or less.

In years when the rains fail to appear, I soak the native plants several times during what should be the rainy season, just to give them a little extra help. It is true that these plants growing out in the wild are not babied in this way, but many do succumb to long-term drought, which for obvious reasons I want to avoid in my garden. Since California is, at the time of this writing, experiencing extreme drought conditions, it is essential for gardeners to conserve water, and so as long as outdoor water use is permitted, I will continue to water mature trees and shrubs as efficiently as possible while withholding water from the lawn and the annual wildflowers. Organic mulch already covers garden beds to reduce evaporation at the surface, and I check sprinklers regularly to make sure they are spraying where intended and not watering the sidewalk. I set the controller to go on when plants begin to

My garden notebook.

show stress, and I always water in the early morning hours, when the winds are calm and the temperature more moderate, making every precious drop count. In place of native perennials that fail to make it through the dry seasons, I will introduce plants that require even less water.

Few weeds grow in my garden because it is dry, the soil is undisturbed, and there is competition from healthy, mature plants. However, I do spend some time removing weeds during late winter and spring, especially in wet years. The garden requires little weeding in summer—a good thing considering how hot it gets here!

Maintaining the parkway wildflowers is labor-intensive. Sowing the seeds in the fall and winter is not much work, but later I have to weed, remove the spent annuals, and collect the seeds to sow for the next season's display.

Sweeping the sidewalk is probably the biggest time sink now that we do not employ a mow-and-blow service. I estimate that I spend on average thirty minutes each week clearing the leaves and debris from sidewalks, paths, and patios.

Each year I also lightly prune the shrubs and trees. In the summer, I remove the low branches from the oaks that obstruct the walkway and street, and I prune branches that are crossed or growing in a way that will be problematic as the trees increase in size. This early corrective pruning is very important for young trees; done properly, the trees will require very little pruning as they mature.

Low-volume, automatic irrigation for my vegetable garden along the driveway.

That is the general overview of my gardening tasks, but the question remains: How much time does all of this take? Well, that depends on whether I'm doing the minimum amount of maintenance or putting in maximum effort. Let's start with a few examples of what minimum care looks like.

We recently spent six months, from December through May, out of the country, during which time the garden received very little attention. We hired a native-plant gardener to come once or twice a month, and she watered the citrus trees and other drought-stressed shrubs, mowed the lawn, and tidied up the yard. Most plants did just fine, in spite of the relative lack of rain during the winter. This year I spent over a month traveling in midsummer, and even though this dry season followed two extremely dry winters, I still only lost one mature shrub, a Ray Hartman California lilac. The California goldenrod growing in the parkway has been very dry and does not look like it will bloom this year; given the drought conditions, I may remove this plant, replacing it with California buckwheat, which requires almost no supplemental water.

Overall, if I had to estimate how much time I spend on routine maintenance, I might say four hours per month on average, although it is not distributed evenly throughout the year. I do little in the garden during the summer and early autumn, but I am busy planting in winter, and weeding and mowing in spring. As with any garden, there are other seasonal tasks, like planting and maintaining vegetable and wildflower gardens, and these take as much time as one wants to devote but are not essential to creating a beautiful and wild suburbia. Finally, as my garden has matured (and I have grown older), the amount of attention and work required has decreased. Not a bad thing at all.

WILD SUBURBIA GARDEN CALENDAR

Season/Task	Frequency
All Year	
Sweep paths and sidewalk	At least weekly
Mow and edge front lawn	Every 3 weeks
Weed new garden beds, being especially vigilant to get Bermuda grass	Apx. 1–2x/month
Cool, Wet Season (November–February)	
Irrigation	
Parkway gardens, oak tree, woodland garden	Usually none; supply if no rain
Front yard, on irrigation system	As needed; apx. 1–2x/month
Backyard avocado, lawn, citrus trees	As needed; apx. 1x/month
Backyard veg. garden, on auto-drip	As needed; apx. 2x/week
Pots	As needed
Weed Control and Pruning	
Prostrate spurge and other winter weeds	1–2x/month
Sow wildflower seeds	2–3x/season
Prune sage and monkeyflowers before new growth begins (late fall)	1x/season
Vigorously prune wild grape after it has gone dormant	1x/season
Vigorously prune hard, mature California fuchsia	1x/seaon
Spring (March–May)	
Irrigation	
Parkway gardens, oak tree, woodland garden	None; water wildflowers to extend bloom
Front yard, on irrigation system	Apx. 2x/month
Backyard avocado, lawn, citrus trees	Apx. 1x/month
Backyard veg. garden, on auto-drip	Apx. 2–3x/week
Pots	As needed

Table continued on the next page.

WILD SUBURBIA GARDEN CALENDAR *cont.*

Season/Task	Frequency
Spring (March–May) *continued*	
Weed Control and Pruning	
Garden spurge, oxalis, warm-season weeds, new beds	Weekly
Weed around, thin, and clear wild-flowers as needed; collect seeds	2–4x/month
Groom large bunchgrasses (e.g., deer grass, alkali sacaton) by raking dried blades with a landscape rake	1x/year
Prune inflorescences from Ray Hart-man California lilac following bloom	1x/year
Prune (tip or pinch back) new growth on sages, monkeyflowers, California fuchsias	As needed
Hot, Dry Season (June–October)	
Irrigation	
Parkway gardens, oak tree, woodland garden	Oak: none; woodland: 1x/month; parkway: 2–3x/season
Front yard, on irrigation system	Apx. 2x/month
Backyard avocado, lawn, citrus trees	As needed; apx. 1–2x/month
Backyard veg. garden, on auto-drip	Daily
Pots	As needed
Pruning	
Prune coast live oak; only remove branches that are dangerous, damaged, crossed, or have narrow crotches, and those whose removal help the tree develop good structure (hire a reputable arborist for mature trees)	As needed; late July to early September
Prune wild grape to control growth; remove from nearby plants and structures	As needed, 2x/month

CONCLUSION:
SIX SUGGESTIONS FOR AVOIDING
THE MOST COMMON MISTAKES

Through the years, I have made—and seen others make—some of the same mistakes over and over again. The following suggestions on planning, design, and planting will hopefully help you avoid these mistakes while you create your dream garden. Remember to:

- Do your homework
- Use more than one of each plant
- Give them room to grow
- Put friends together
- Work with Mother Nature
- Try, try again

DO YOUR HOMEWORK

It is very difficult for plant or landscape experts to help if they lack a clear understanding of your garden conditions, the kind of garden you want, and how much work you want to do. Plan before you go to the nursery or plant sale. Spend time observing your yard and visiting others. Attend classes and garden tours, and talk with people whose gardens you admire. Develop a clear sense of the type of garden you want to work toward, and when you're finally ready to go shopping, take along pictures of your own yard and of gardens that inspire you. Don't miss the plant sales of local chapters of the California Native Plant Society, where you will have access to not only great plants but also expert advice, interesting talks, and nice people who share your interest in our remarkable native flora.

USE MORE THAN ONE OF EACH PLANT

As plant lovers, it can be hard to resist trying lots of new and unusual plants. I must confess I am guilty of making this mistake: "Oh, that looks so cute. Can't you just see it in my garden?" If I follow through

There is no order to the planting of these coastal sage scrub plants: no repetition, no break, etc. This creates an unappealing, chaotic look.

and buy the plant, I risk my garden looking like a chaotic mishmash. I became aware of this tendency while visiting the garden of a friend who is a landscape architect. Throughout her garden were clusters of the striking white Canyon Snow variety of iris. In contrast, my yard was randomly scattered with irises bearing names like "Gold & Maroon," "Plum & Yellow," and "Oxymoron"—their names as colorful as their blooms. One garden is a hodgepodge of plants; the other, a relaxing, pleasant, and natural-looking arrangement. Follow my friend's example and try to mesh your love of plants with good design principles.

GIVE THEM ROOM TO GROW

Crowding plants is a very common mistake made by professionals and amateurs alike. Many native plants look scrawny in one-gallon pots, but remember that they adapt best when planted young, and they grow quickly once established. Sugar bush, for example, can look like a stick in a one-gallon pot, but in five years it may grow to four feet in height and width, and its mature size can exceed ten feet by ten feet.

Placing plants too close to paths and sidewalks is also a problem and can lead to years of maintenance, unappealing sheared edges, and potentially dangerous tripping hazards. Look up as well to make sure that trees have room to reach their full heights. Heavy pruning of large trees is expensive and usually results in structural and health problems for the tree, so it pays to plant them wisely in the first place.

Although it can be hard to space young plants far enough apart that they can reach their mature size without bumping into other plants, this is just what you must do for a beautiful and easy-to-maintain garden. Do not rely on your eye; measure it out. If the label says that a plant will grow to six feet in width, do not plant anything permanent within the six-foot circle that it will ultimately fill.

Sage planted too close to the sidewalk requires ongoing shearing. This is bad for the sages, it generates excess green waste, it wastes labor, and it looks bad.

Professionals often crowd plants so that their customers are pleased with their new gardens during the first couple of years, but that is not a good long-term plan. Remember: gardening teaches us patience. Resist overcrowding so that your garden will be at its best for many years to come.

PUT FRIENDS TOGETHER

You may love the way the yellow flowers of one shrub look with the blue flowers of a groundcover, but if these plants have different needs, do not put them together. If you are going to keep some lawn or high-water-use plantings, select plants that will accept the extra water and serve to transition to the drier adjacent beds. Observe plants in their natural settings to see which ones grow together; these plants will have similar needs and form a natural-looking association.

Liquidambar trees will never be the right choice for under power lines.

Oak trees are too large for these small parking lot islands. The low-growing shrubs are toyon, an upright evergreen shrub. Both plants will require constant pruning and are likely to suffer from being so constrained.

These Canary Island pines will never recover from the butchering they suffered. Select trees whose mature sizes match the desired landscape scale.

WORK WITH MOTHER NATURE

The most successful gardens are those that work with nature rather than try to overcome it. Get to know where your plants naturally grow, and try to mimic those conditions. Keep in mind, however, that young plants will need more water than established plants you find in the wild, especially during the hot, dry summer. Winter is the best time of year to transfer new additions to your garden because the rainy season (and a little extra watering from you) will help them transition from their early life in nursery containers to their new permanent homes. Keep an eye on these young plants and water them deeply before they show signs of stress. To keep them hydrated, water early in the day or, if possible, on foggy days, when the soil is cool. Once they are established (usually after two or three summers), water them during dry winters and occasionally during the summer to keep them more verdant than they might be out in the wild. The rule of thumb is to water thoroughly but infrequently.

TRY, TRY AGAIN

Above all, remember that gardening is a process, and it should be an enjoyable one. The most successful gardeners stick with it, learning from their mistakes and celebrating their successes. You don't need to be perfect, just determined.

GARDEN INTERLUDE: WILD SUBURBIA TODAY

The drive home is long and slow. The radio announcer reports on another major catastrophe. I turn off the car, step out, and open the gate to my back yard. I take a deep, refreshing breath. My eyes scan the yard and see birds, butterflies, and dragonflies flitting around. I look to see what is blooming, ignoring the weeds and grass creeping through the rock border.

When I moved into this century-old house, the yard was dominated by thirsty lawn, and the garden was quiet. Few birds found food or solace in my green desert. Gradually over the past fifteen years I've replaced the lawn with water-saving native plants. The result has been dramatic. My water bill declines with the removal of each square foot of grass, and the diversity of plants attracts all kinds of interesting critters.

Each year I look forward to the burst of spring wildflowers in the planted strip along the sidewalk beside my house. The blues of the sages, ceanothus, and penstemons calm me, while the bright orange and red of the mallows and monkeyflowers quicken my pulse. The coolness of the woodland garden with its rich, deep greens is a comforting sight.

Even the compost heap is interesting: it is the wildest wilderness of my suburbia, teeming with life, with hunters, grazers, scavengers, and

decomposers. They take the form of mammals, lizards, insects, snakes, spiders, and unknowns. It is my favorite garden spot.

The city, as I suspected, did not want to cite me for failure to comply with the landscape ordinance for parkways. A complaint was filed by an anonymous stranger, and the city just followed its protocol. The parkway plants remain taller than the twelve-inch height restriction, although my removal of the seven-foot-tall Frosty Blue California lilac was a coincidental step toward compliance. Recently I was asked to come to a city commission meeting to discuss the parkway ordinance. I shared my thoughts on why lawn was not the best solution for these strips, and although the original ordinance has since been changed, I am pretty sure I am still out of compliance. For now, however, especially given the current severe drought conditions, the city has no interest in enforcing these rules.

Parkway gardens, including some with native plants, continue to spring up throughout the city. I removed the lawn from the eighty-foot-long grassy parkway in front of my house, so now all of the parkway area (over one thousand square feet) surrounding our corner lot is lawn-free. The front parkway garden still looks a bit scraggly with its mounds of rocks and native bunchgrasses, but I plan to fill it in with lots of new plants.

The side parkway was my first big native plant garden project, and I learned many things from it. First, I should have believed the label on the Frosty Blue California lilac. Yes, it was well adapted to garden conditions and it seemed to love my loamy soil. And yes, it does grow to six to eight feet in height, and even wider than that. The parkway is only six feet wide, meaning that I've spent too much time trying to keep that plant in bounds.

This was definitely a mistake, although when it was gloriously blooming, I did love it.

Similarly, some of the bunchgrasses that I planted are now too large for the space. The deer grass and alkali sacaton are lovely plants, but I should have given them more room and placed them farther from the sidewalk. In the future I plan to dig out and divide the older grasses and replant them with better placement. My gardens will always be works in progress.

And finally, I should have left more room for people to cross from the sidewalk to the street. Again, as I rejuvenate the bunchgrasses, I will leave space for flagstones that will allow for easy passage. Then, people will be able to walk beside my garden and also through it.

Nevertheless, the garden has been a big success. I love spending time with my plants, and my neighbors stop by when I am outside gardening to tell me how much they enjoy what I have done. Some say the garden reminds them of the nearby mountains—a bit of untamed nature springing up in an otherwise orderly subdivision. I find this especially gratifying at the end of our hot, dry season, when the bright colors of spring and summer have faded into grays and tans; I am not the only one who sees the beauty in California's native flora. People slow down, watch butterflies, and breathe more deeply here. It is my Wild Suburbia, but I am happy to share it with everyone.

T HE PLANT LISTS in Appendices A through D are alphabetized under type by common name. There is no formal system for the assignment of these names, but I tried to select the names most frequently used. The botanical names that follow conform to the Jepson Online Interchange. Due to advances in our understanding of plant taxonomy, there have been many modifications in scientific nomenclature, and here, the plant names that have recently changed are listed with their former genus names in brackets, since many gardeners and growers continue to use these earlier designations.

NATIVE PLANTS FOR SUMMER-DRY (CHAPARRAL OR SCRUB) GARDENS

The plants on this list typically grow in chaparral or sage scrub communities. They require little summer water after establishment. Be sure to water during dry winters to help the plants survive the long, hot dry season.

SHRUBS

bigberry manzanita (*Arctostaphylos glauca*)

black sage (*Salvia mellifera*)

bladderpod (*Peritoma* [formerly *Isomeris*] *arborea*)

blue elderberry (*Sambucus nigra* [formerly *S. Mexicana*] ssp. *cerulea*)

California buckwheat (*Eriogonum fasciculatum*)

California encelia (*Encelia californica*)

California sagebrush (*Artemisia californica*)

Catalina cherry (*Prunus ilicifolia* ssp. *lyonii*)

Channel Island tree poppy (*Dendromecon harfordii*)

chaparral whitethorn (*Ceanothus leucodermis*)

Cleveland sage (*Salvia clevelandii*)

coyote brush (*Baccharis pilularis*)

Golden Abundance barberry (*Berberis* [formerly *Mahonia*] 'Golden Abundance')

holly-leafed cherry (*Prunus ilicifolia*)

Howard McMinn manzanita (*Arctostaphylos* 'Howard McMinn')

laurel sumac (*Malosma laurina*)

Matilija poppy (*Romneya coulteri*)

mountain mahogany (*Cercocarpus betuloides*)

Nevin's barberry (*Berberis* [formerly *Mahonia*] *nevinii*)

purple sage (*Salvia leucophylla*)

red-flowered buckwheat (*Eriogonum grande* var. *rubescens*)

St. Catherine's lace (*Eriogonum giganteum*)
sugar bush (*Rhus ovata*)
toyon (*Heteromeles arbutifolia*)
white sage (*Salvia apiana*)
woolly bluecurls (*Trichostema lanatum*)

PERENNIALS
California fuchsia (*Epilobium* [formerly *Zauschneria*] species and cultivars)
Canyon Prince giant wild rye (*Elymus* [formerly *Leymus*] *condensatus* 'Canyon Prince')
common yarrow (*Achillea millefolium*)
David's Choice sandhill sagebrush (*Artemisia pycnocephala* 'David's Choice')
De La Mina lilac verbena (*Verbena lilacina* 'De La Mina')
deer grass (*Muhlenbergia rigens*)

Margarita BOP penstemon (*Penstemon heterophyllus* 'Margarita BOP')
monkeyflower (*Mimulus* species and cultivars)
narrow-leaf milkweed (*Asclepias fascicularis*)
purple needlegrass (*Stipa* [formerly *Nassella*] *pulchra*)

GROUNDCOVERS
Bee's Bliss sage (*Salvia* 'Bee's Bliss')
Island Pink yarrow (*Achillea millefolium* 'Island Pink')
Pigeon Point coyote brush (*Baccharis pilularis* 'Pigeon Point')
San Diego marsh-elder (*Iva hayesiana*)

VINES
Anacapa Pink California morning glory (*Calystegia macrostegia* ssp. *macrostegia* 'Anacapa Pink')

NATIVE PLANTS FOR MOIST GARDENS
These plants, selected from riparian woodland environments, need year-round moisture and usually grow in organically rich soils.

TREES
big-leaf maple (*Acer macrophyllum*)
black cottonwood (*Populus trichocarpa*)
black willow (*Salix gooddingii*)
California bay (*Umbellularia californica*)
Fremont cottonwood (*Populus fremontii*)
western sycamore (*Platanus racemosa*)
white alder (*Alnus rhombifolia*)

SHRUBS
American dogwood (*Cornus sericea*)
arroyo willow (*Salix lasiolepis*)
bearberry (*Arctostaphylos uva-ursi*)
bush anemone (*Carpenteria californica*)
buttonbush (*Cephalanthus occidentalis* var. *californicus*)
canyon sunflower (*Venegasia carpesioides*)
Catalina perfume (*Ribes viburnifolium*)
chaparral currant (*Ribes malvaceum*)

creeping barberry (*Berberis* [formerly *Mahonia*] *aquifolium* var. *repens*)

fuchsia-flowering gooseberry (*Ribes speciosum*)

Golden Abundance barberry (*Berberis* [formerly *Mahonia*] 'Golden Abundance')

hillside gooseberry (*Ribes californicum*)

mule fat (*Baccharis salicifolia*)

narrow-leaved willow (*Salix exigua*)

Oregon grape (*Berberis* [formerly *Mahonia*] *aquifolium*)

Pacific ninebark (*Physocarpus capitatus*)

Pacific wax myrtle (*Morella* [formerly *Myrica*] *californica*)

Pacific willow (*Salix lasiandra* var. *lasiandra*)

red flowering currant (*Ribes sanguineum*)

salal (*Gaultheria shallon*)

twinberry (*Lonicera involucrata*)

vine maple (*Acer circinatum*)

western choke-cherry (*Prunus virginiana*)

western hazelnut (*Corylus cornuta* var. *californica*)

wild mock orange (*Philadelphus lewisii*)

yerba buena (*Clinopodium* [formerly *Satureja*] *douglasii*)

PERENNIALS

California polypody (*Polypodium californicum*)

California sea pink (*Armeria maritima*)

California wood strawberry (*Fragaria vesca*)

Canyon Prince giant wild rye (*Leymus* [formerly *Elymus*] *condensatus* 'Canyon Prince')

coastal wood fern (*Dryopteris arguta*)

common yarrow (*Achillea millefolium*)

coral bells (*Heuchera* species and cultivars)

deer fern (*Blechnum spicant*)

giant chain fern (*Woodwardia fimbriata*)

gray rush (*Juncus patens*)

heartleaf keckiella (*Keckiella cordifolia*)

hummingbird sage (*Salvia spathacea*)

island alum root (*Heuchera maxima*)

meadow rue (*Thalictrum fendleri* var. *polycarpum* [formerly *T. polycarpum*])

mugwort (*Artemisia douglasiana*)

red fescue (*Festuca rubra*)

scarlet monkeyflower (*Mimulus cardinalis*)

seaside daisy (*Erigeron glaucus*)

sedge (*Carex* species and cultivars)

seep monkeyflower (*Mimulus guttatus*)

southern goldenrod (*Solidago confinis*)

W. R. seaside daisy (*Erigeron* 'W. R.')

western columbine (*Aquilegia formosa*)

western sword fern (*Polystichum munitum*)

yerba mansa (*Anemopsis californica*)

VINES

California wild grape (*Vitis californica*)

Roger's Red grape (*Vitis* 'Roger's Red')

virgin's bower (*Clematis ligusticifolia*)

NATIVE PLANTS FOR HOT, DRY GARDENS

Appropriate for dry gardens, many of these desert plants will bloom if watered occasionally during the summer to mimic natural monsoonal rain conditions. These plants generally require good drainage and are not well adapted to summer fog and winter rains; make sure you select plants that are hardy to your winter conditions.

TREES

blue palo verde (*Cercidium floridum*)

Desert Museum Palo Verde (*Parkinsonia* 'Desert Museum')

desert willow (*Chilopsis linearis*)

ironwood (*Olneya tesota*)

Joshua tree (*Yucca brevifolia*)

pinyon pine (*Pinus monophylla*)

SHRUBS

Apache plume (*Fallugia paradoxa*)

apricot mallow (*Sphaeralcea ambigua*)

big saltbush (*Atriplex lentiformis*)

brittlebush (*Encelia farinosa*)

California juniper (*Juniperus californica*)

catclaw (*Acacia greggii*)

chuparosa (*Justicia* [formerly *Beloperone*] *californica*)

creosote bush (*Larrea tridentata*)

desert barberry (*Berberis* [formerly *Mahonia*] *haematocarpa*)

desert lavender (*Condea* [formerly *Hyptis*] *emoryi*)

desert sage (*Salvia dorrii*)

desert tea (*Ephedra californica*)

fourwing saltbush (*Atriplex canescens*)

grape soda lupine (*Lupinus excubitus*)

Great Basin sagebrush (*Artemisia tridentata*)

interior goldenbush (*Ericameria linearifolia*)

jojoba (*Simmondsia chinensis*)

mesquite (*Prosopis glandulosa*)

Mormon tea (*Ephedra nevadensis*)

Palmer's mallow (*Abutilon palmeri*)

pink fairy duster (*Calliandra eriophylla*)

rabbit bush (*Ericameria* [formerly *Chrysothamnus*] *nauseosus*)

screw bean (*Prosopis pubescens*)

yellow bush snapdragon (*Keckiella antirrhinoides*)

PERENNIALS

alkali sacaton (*Sporobolus airoides*)

California evening primrose (*Oenothera californica*)

desert four-o'clock (*Mirabilis multiflora* var. *pubescens*)

desert marigold (*Baileya multiradiata*)

desert needlegrass (*Stipa* [formerly *Achnatherum*] *speciosa*)

Eaton's firecracker penstemon (*Penstemon eatonii*)

fragrant evening primrose
(*Oenothera caespitosa*)
sand rice-grass (*Stipa* [formerly
Achnatherum] *hymenoides*)

SUCCULENTS
banana yucca (*Yucca baccata*)
beargrass (*Nolina bigelovii*)
beavertail cactus (*Opuntia basilaris*)

desert century plant (*Agave deserti*)
Mojave yucca (*Yucca schidigera*)
ocotillo (*Fouquieria splendens*)
Parry beargrass (*Nolina parryi*)
Shaw agave (*Agave shawii*)
Utah agave (*Agave utahensis*)

VINES
desert wild grape (*Vitis girdiana*)

NATIVE PLANTS FOR UNDER EVERGREEN OAKS

These selections need part shade and little summer water, so they're a perfect fit for planting under evergreen oaks. The most important consideration when planting near a mature tree is maintaining the health of the tree, so aim to disturb the soil as little as possible during planting, keep summer water to a minimum, and plant as far from the base of the tree as you can.

SHRUBS
bush anemone (*Carpenteria
californica*)
California rose (*Rosa californica*)
canyon sunflower (*Venegasia
carpesioides*)
Catalina perfume (*Ribes
viburnifolium*)
chaparral currant (*Ribes
malvaceum*)
coffeeberry (*Frangula* [formerly
Rhamnus] *californica*)
creeping barberry (*Berberis*
[formerly *Mahonia*] *aquifolium*
var. *repens*)
fuchsia-flowering gooseberry
(*Ribes speciosum*)
Golden Abundance barberry
(*Berberis* [formerly *Mahonia*]
'Golden Abundance')
holly-leaved cherry (*Prunus
ilicifolia*)

Nevin's barberry (*Berberis* [formerly
Mahonia] *nevinii*)
Oregon grape (*Berberis* [formerly
Mahonia] *aquifolium*)
red flowering currant (*Ribes
sanguineum*)
spiny redberry (*Rhamnus crocea*)
toyon (*Heteromeles arbutifolia*)
yerba buena (*Clinopodium
[formerly Satureja*] *douglasii*)

PERENNIALS
California fescue (*Festuca
californica*)
California polypody (*Polypodium
californicum*)
California wood strawberry
(*Fragaria vesca* [formerly *F. vesca*
ssp. *californica*])
Canyon Prince giant wild rye
(*Elymus* [formerly *Leymus*]
condensatus 'Canyon Prince')
coast melic grass (*Melica
imperfecta*)

coastal wood fern (*Dryopteris arguta*)

coral bells (*Heuchera* species and cultivars)

Douglas iris (*Iris douglasiana*)

giant chain fern (*Woodwardia fimbriata*)

heartleaf keckiella (*Keckiella cordifolia*)

hummingbird sage (*Salvia spathacea*)

island alum root (*Heuchera maxima*)

meadow rue (*Thalictrum fendleri* var. *polycarpum* [formerly *T. polycarpum*])

western brackenfern (*Pteridium aquilinum*)

western columbine (*Aquilegia formosa*)

wire grass (*Juncus patens*)

VINES

California Dutchman's pipe (*Aristolochia californica*)

pipestems (*Clematis lasiantha*)

virgin's bower (*Clematis ligusticifolia*)

NATIVE PLANTS FOR COASTAL GARDENS WITH SANDY SOIL

These plants prefer excellent drainage and lean soils. Use organic mulch to help soil fertility and structure improve over time.

SHRUBS

ashyleaf buckwheat (*Eriogonum cinereum*)

Baja bush snapdragon (*Gambelia* [formerly *Galvezia*] *juncea*)

big saltbush (*Atriplex lentiformis*)

bladderpod (*Peritoma* [formerly *Isomeris*] *arborea*)

Brandegee's sage (*Salvia brandegeei*)

California buckwheat (*Eriogonum fasciculatum*)

Canyon Gray sagebrush (*Artemisia californica* 'Canyon Gray')

coyote brush (*Baccharis pilularis*)

desert lavender (*Condea* [formerly *Hyptis*] *emoryi*)

giant coreopsis (*Leptosyne* [formerly *Coreopsis*] *gigantea*)

island tree mallow (*Lavatera assurgentiflora*)

lemonade berry (*Rhus integrifolia*)

Little Sur manzanita (*Arctostaphylos edmundsii* 'Little Sur')

Point Sal Spreader sage (*Salvia leucophylla* 'Point Sal Spreader')

purple sage (*Salvia leucophylla*)

tree lupine (*Lupinus arboreus*)

PERENNIALS

beach evening primrose (*Camissonia cheiranthifolia*)

beach strawberry (*Fragaria chiloensis*)

California sea pink (*Armeria maritima*)

Canyon Prince giant wild rye (*Elymus* [formerly *Leymus*] *condensatus* 'Canyon Prince')

clustered field sedge (*Carex praegracilis*)

coast aster (*Symphyotrichum chilense* [formerly *Aster chilensis*])

coast buckwheat (*Eriogonum latifolium*)

coast wallflower (*Erysimum menziesii*)

common yarrow (*Achillea millefolium*)

David's Choice sandhill sagebrush (*Artemisia pycnocephala* 'David's Choice')

dune bent grass (*Agrostis pallens*)

dune sedge (*Carex pansa*)

dune tansy (*Tanacetum bipinnatum* [formerly *T. camphoratum*])

sand verbena (*Abronia maritima*)

sea dahlia (*Leptosyne* [formerly *Coreopsis*] *maritima*)

seaside daisy (*Erigeron glaucus*)

seaside golden yarrow (*Eriophyllum staechadifolium*)

spreading gum plant (*Grindelia stricta* var. *platyphylla*)

GROUNDCOVERS

maritime ceanothus (*Ceanothus maritimus*)

Point St. George aster (*Symphyotrichum chilense* [formerly *Aster chilensis*] 'Point St. George')

San Diego marsh-elder (*Iva hayesiana*)

Silver Carpet California aster (*Corethrogyne* [formerly *Lessingia*] *filaginifolia* 'Silver Carpet')

NATIVE PLANTS FOR HEAVY CLAY SOIL

The following plants are better adapted to the challenging conditions created by heavy, poorly drained soil. Soil structure and drainage will improve as the garden matures.

TREES

big-leaf maple (*Acer macrophyllum*)

chaparral flowering ash (*Fraxinus dipetala*)

coast live oak (*Quercus agrifolia*)

Coulter pine (*Pinus coulteri*)

cutleaf tanbark oak (*Notholithocarpus* [formerly *Lithocarpus*] *densiflorus*)

desert willow (*Chilopsis linearis*)

Engelmann oak (*Quercus engelmannii*)

foothill pine (*Pinus sabiniana*)

incense cedar (*Calocedrus decurrens*)

knobcone pine (*Pinus attenuata*)

Lawson cypress (*Chamaecyparis lawsoniana*)

Tecate cypress (*Cupressus forbesii*)

Torrey pine (*Pinus torreyana*)

valley oak (*Quercus lobata*)

white alder (*Alnus rhombifolia*)

SHRUBS

barberry (*Berberis* [formerly *Mahonia*] *pinnata*)

bladderpod (*Peritoma* [formerly *Isomeris*] *arborea*)

California juniper (*Juniperus californica*)

California rose (*Rosa californica*)

Canyon Silver island snowflake
(*Constancea* [formerly
Eriophyllum] *nevinii* 'Canyon
Silver')
chaparral honeysuckle (*Lonicera
interrupta*)
coffeeberry (*Frangula* [formerly
Rhamnus] *californica*)
creeping barberry (*Berberis*
[formerly *Mahonia*] *aquifolia*
var. *repens*)
desert olive (*Forestiera pubescens*)
Fremont barberry (*Berberis*
formerly *Mahonia*] *fremontii*)
Golden Abundance barberry
(*Berberis* [formerly *Mahonia*]
'Golden Abundance')
island tree mallow (*Lavatera
assurgentiflora*)
Leyland cypress (x *Cuprocyparis
leylandii*)
Nevin's barberry (*Berberis*
[formerly *Mahonia*] *nevinii*)
Oregon grape (*Berberis* [formerly
Mahonia] *aquifolium*)
twinberry (*Lonicera involucrata*)
western redbud (*Cercis
occidentalis*)
yerba buena (*Clinopodium*
[formerly *Satureja*] *douglasii*)

PERENNIALS
beach strawberry (*Fragaria
chiloensis*)
blue-eyed grass (*Sisyrinchium
bellum*)
California buttercup (*Ranunculus
californicus*)
California fuchsia (*Epilobium*
[formerly *Zauschneria*] species
and cultivars)

California goldenrod (*Solidago
velutina* ssp. *californica*
[formerly *S. californica*])
California polypody (*Polypodium
californicum*)
common yarrow (*Achillea
millefolium*)
deer grass (*Muhlenbergia rigens*)
fleabane (*Erigeron* species and
cultivars)
foothill needlegrass (*Stipa*
[formerly *Nassella*] *lepida*)
foothill penstemon (*Penstemon
heterophyllus*)
fringe cup (*Tellima grandiflora*)
giant chain fern (*Woodwardia
fimbriata*)
golden yarrow (*Eriophyllum
confertiflorum*)
gumplant (*Grindelia robusta*)
heartleaf keckiella (*Keckiella
cordifolia*)
Hooker's evening primrose
(*Oenothera elata* ssp. *hookeri*)
hummingbird sage (*Salvia
spathacea*)
island alum root (*Heuchera
maxima*)
meadow rue (*Thalictrum fendleri*
var. *polycarpum* [formerly
T. polycarpum])
nodding needlegrass (*Stipa*
[formerly *Nassella*] *cernua*)
purple needlegrass (*Stipa* [formerly
Nassella] *pulchra*)
Sarah Lyman polypody fern
(*Polypodium californicum*
'Sarah Lyman')
scarlet monkeyflower (*Mimulus
cardinalis*)

sea dahlia (*Leptosyne* [formerly *Coreopsis*] *maritima*)
seaside daisy (*Erigeron glaucus*)
showy penstemon (*Penstemon spectabilis*)
Southern bush monkeyflower (*Mimulus aurantiacus* [formerly *M. longiflorus*])
wire grass (*Juncus patens*)

GROUNDCOVERS
San Diego marsh-elder (*Iva hayesiana*)

SUCCULENTS
chaparral yucca (*Hesperoyucca* [formerly *Yucca*] *whipplei*)
Parry beargrass (*Nolina parryi*)

BULBS
blue dicks (*Dichelostemma pulchellum*)
Ithuriel's Spear (*Triteleia laxa*)
soap plant (*Chlorogalum pomeridianum*)

COLORFUL FILLER PLANTS FOR YOUNG GARDENS

Though some of these plants may be short-lived, they fill out and bloom within the first year, making them perfect for new gardens. Be sure to clear perennial and annual (wildflower) filler plants away from slower-growing, more permanent perennials.

SHRUBS
Palmer's mallow (*Abutilon palmeri*)
red-flowered buckwheat (*Eriogonum grande* var. *rubescens*)
Winnifred Gilman Cleveland sage (*Salvia clevelandii* 'Winnifred Gilman')

PERENNIALS
blue flax (*Linum lewisii*)
California fuchsia (*Epilobium* [formerly *Zauschneria*] species and cultivars)
California sea pink (*Armeria maritima*)
common yarrow (*Achillea millefolium*)
coral bells (*Heuchera* species and cultivars)
De La Mina lilac verbena (*Verbena lilacina* 'De La Mina')

hummingbird sage (*Salvia spathacea*)
Margarita BOP penstemon (*Penstemon heterophyllus* 'Margarita BOP')
monkeyflower (*Mimulus* species and cultivars)

GROUNDCOVERS
Island Pink yarrow (*Achillea millefolium* 'Island Pink')
Silver Carpet California aster (*Corethrogyne* [formerly *Lessingia*] *filaginifolia* 'Silver Carpet')

ANNUALS
California poppy (*Eschscholzia californica*)
sunflower (*Helianthus annuus*)
California wildflower mix

LOW-GROWING NATIVE PLANTS FOR PARKWAYS

This list includes low-growing, tough plants for parkways. Check with your city on landscape ordinance regulations before planting.

SHRUBS

Anchor Bay Pt. Reyes California lilac (*Ceanothus gloriosus* 'Anchor Bay')

ashyleaf buckwheat (*Eriogonum cinereum*)

bearberry (*Arctostaphylos uva-ursi*)

Canyon Gray sagebrush (*Artemisia californica* 'Canyon Gray')

Catalina perfume (*Ribes viburnifolium*)

creeping barberry (*Berberis* [formerly *Mahonia*] *aquifolia* var. *repens*)

Emerald Carpet manzanita (*Arctostaphylos* 'Emerald Carpet')

Mrs. Beard sage (*Salvia* 'Mrs. Beard')

PERENNIALS

alkali sacaton (*Sporobolus airoides*)

Arthur Menzies seaside daisy (*Erigeron glaucus* 'Arthur Menzies')

beach strawberry (*Fragaria chiloensis*)

blue flax (*Linum lewisii*)

blue grama (*Bouteloua gracilis*)

blue-eyed grass (*Sisyrinchium bellum*)

Bountiful seaside daisy (*Erigeron glaucus* 'Bountiful')

California evening primrose (*Oenothera californica*)

California fescue (*Festuca californica*)

California fuchsia (*Epilobium* [formerly *Zauschneria*] *canum*)

California mint (*Pycnanthemum californicum*)

California sea pink (*Armeria maritima*)

California wood strawberry (*Fragaria vesca*)

Canyon Prince giant wild rye (*Elymus* [formerly *Leymus*] *condensatus* 'Canyon Prince')

Canyon Snow Douglas iris (*Iris douglasiana* 'Canyon Snow')

common yarrow (*Achillea millefolium*)

coral bells (*Heuchera* species and cultivars)

creeping sage (*Salvia sonomensis*)

Dara's Choice sage (*Salvia* 'Dara's Choice')

David's Choice sandhill sagebrush (*Artemisia pycnocephala* 'David's Choice')

deer grass (*Muhlenbergia rigens*)

desert four-o'clock (*Mirabilis multiflora* var. *pubescens*)

desert marigold (*Baileya multiradiata*)

Douglas iris (*Iris douglasiana*)

El Tigre California fuchsia (*Epilobium* [formerly *Zauschneria*] *canum* 'El Tigre')

foothill needlegrass (*Stipa* [formerly *Nassella*] *lepida*)

foothill penstemon (*Penstemon heterophyllus*)

fragrant evening primrose (*Oenothera caespitosa*)

hummingbird sage (*Salvia spathacea*)
Idaho fescue (*Festuca idahoensis*)
Margarita BOP penstemon (*Penstemon heterophyllus* 'Margarita BOP')
nodding needlegrass (*Stipa* [formerly *Nassella*] *cernua*)
oniongrass (*Melica imperfecta*)
Pacific Coast Hybrid iris (*Iris*–PCH)
peak rush rose (*Crocanthemum* [formerly *Helianthemum*] *scoparium*)
purple needlegrass (*Stipa* [formerly *Nassella*] *pulchra*)
purple three-awn (*Aristida purpurea* var. *purpurea*)
rush (*Juncus* species and cultivars)
San Bruno Mountain golden aster (*Heterotheca* [formerly *Chrysopsis*] *sessiliflora* ssp. *Bolanderi* 'San Bruno Mountain')
Sea Breeze seaside daisy (*Erigeron glaucus* 'Sea Breeze')
sedge (*Carex* species and cultivars)
Shasta Sulphur buckwheat (*Eriogonum umbellatum* var. *polyanthum* 'Shasta Sulphur')
southern goldenrod (*Solidago confinis*)
W. R. seaside daisy (*Erigeron* 'W. R.')
Warriner Lytle California buckwheat (*Eriogonum fasciculatum* 'Warriner Lytle')

wishbone bush (*Mirabilis californica*)
yerba mansa (*Anemopsis californica*)

GROUNDCOVERS

Bee's Bliss sage (*Salvia* 'Bee's Bliss')
frogfruit (*Phyla nodiflora*)
Island Pink yarrow (*Achillea millefolium* 'Island Pink')
Little Sur manzanita (*Arctostaphylos edmundsii* 'Little Sur')
maritime California lilac (*Ceanothus maritimus*)
Pigeon Point coyote brush (*Baccharis pilularis* 'Pigeon Point')
Point St. George aster (*Symphyotrichum chilense* [formerly *Aster chilensis*] 'Point St. George')
San Diego marsh elder (*Iva hayesiana*)
Silver Carpet California aster (*Corethrogyne* [formerly *Lessingia*] *filaginifolia* 'Silver Carpet')
Yankee Point California lilac (*Ceanothus thyrsiflorus* var. *griseus* 'Yankee Point')

SUCCULENTS

Catalina Island live-forever (*Dudleya virens* ssp. *hassei*)

ANNUALS

California poppy (*Eschscholzia californica*)

APPENDIX B
PLANTS IN THE AUTHOR'S WILD SUBURBAN GARDEN

THESE ARE THE trees, shrubs, perennials, and wildflowers growing in the author's South Pasadena garden.

TREES
boojum tree (*Idria columnaris*)
coast live oak (*Quercus agrifolia*)

SHRUBS
apricot mallow (*Sphaeralcea ambigua*)
Baja bush snapdragon (*Gambelia* [formerly *Galvezia*] *juncea*)
bigleaf crownbeard (*Verbesina dissita*)
bladderpod (*Peritoma* [formerly *Isomeris*] *arborea*)
Brandegee's sage hybrid (*Salvia brandegeei* x *munzii*)
bush anemone (*Carpenteria californica*)
California buckwheat (*Eriogonum fasciculatum* var. *poliofolium*)
California buckwheat (*Eriogonum fasciculatum*)
California copperleaf (*Acalypha californica*)
California Glory flannelbush (*Fremontodendron* 'California Glory')
California sagebrush (*Artemisia californica*)
Catalina perfume (*Ribes viburnifolium*)
Channel Island tree poppy (*Dendromecon harfordii*)

coffeeberry (*Frangula* [formerly *Rhamnus*] *californica*)
common manzanita (*Arctostaphylos manzanita*)
creeping barberry (*Berberis* [formerly *Mahonia*] *repens*)
creeping snowberry (*Symphoricarpos mollis*)
Davis Gold toyon (*Heteromeles arbutifolia* 'Davis Gold')
Emerald Cascade Munz's sage (*Salvia munzii* 'Emerald Cascade')
Eve Case coffeeberry (*Frangula* [formerly *Rhamnus*] *californica* 'Eve Case')
fuchsia-flowering gooseberry (*Ribes speciosum*)
goldenbush (*Isocoma menziesii*)
holly-leafed cherry (*Prunus ilicifolia*)
Lester Rowntree manzanita (*Arctostaphylos* 'Lester Rowntree')
Louis Edmunds California lilac (*Ceanothus thyrsiflorus* var. *griseus* 'Louis Edmunds')
Palmer's mallow (*Abutilon palmeri*)
Pozo Blue sage (*Salvia* 'Pozo Blue')
Ray Hartman California lilac (*Ceanothus* 'Ray Hartman')
San Gabriel flannelbush (*Fremontodendron* 'San Gabriel')

Schoener's Nutkana rose (*Rosa* 'Schoener's Nutkana')
Sentinel manzanita (*Arctostaphylos* 'Sentinel')
Skylark barberry (*Berberis* [formerly *Mahonia*] 'Skylark')
spice bush (*Calycanthus occidentalis*)
Tilden Park snowberry (*Symphoricarpos albus* var. *laevigatus* 'Tilden Park')
toyon (*Heteromeles arbutifolia*)
Twin Peaks #2 coyote brush (*Baccharis pilularis* var. *pilularis* 'Twin Peaks #2')
Utah serviceberry (*Amelanchier utahensis*)
white sage (*Salvia apiana*)
Winnifred Gilman Cleveland sage (*Salvia clevelandii* 'Winnifred Gilman')

PERENNIALS
alkali sacaton (*Sporobolus airoides*)
beach strawberry (*Fragaria chiloensis*)
blue grama (*Bouteloua gracilis*)
blue-eyed grass (*Sisyrinchium bellum*)
bush monkeyflower (*Mimulus aurantiacus*)
California fescue (*Festuca californica*)
California fuchsia (*Epilobium* [formerly *Zauschneria*] *canum*)
California goldenrod (*Solidago velutina* ssp. *californica* [formerly *S. californica*])
cane bluestem (*Bothriochloa barbinodis*)

Carman's Gray rush (*Juncus patens* 'Carman's Gray')
clustered field sedge (*Carex praegracilis*)
De La Mina lilac verbena (*Verbena lilacina* 'De La Mina')
deer grass (*Muhlenbergia rigens*)
desert four-o'clock (*Mirabilis multiflora* var. *pubescens*)
Dorothea's Ruby iris (*Iris* 'Dorothea's Ruby')
Douglas iris (*Iris douglasiana*)
Eleanor monkeyflower (*Mimulus* 'Eleanor')
Elk Blue rush (*Juncus patens* 'Elk Blue')
heartleaf keckiella (*Keckiella cordifolia*)
hummingbird sage (*Salvia spathacea*)
Margarita BOP penstemon (*Penstemon heterophyllus* 'Margarita BOP')
meadow rue (*Thalictrum fendleri* var. *polycarpum* [formerly *T. polycarpum*])
monkeyflower (*Mimulus* species and cultivars)
mugwort (*Artemisia douglasiana*)
needlegrass (*Stipa* [formerly *Nassella*] species)
oniongrass (*Melica imperfecta*)
Pacific Coast Hybrid iris (*Iris*–PCH)
Palmer's senecio (*Senecio palmeri*)
purple three-awn (*Aristida purpurea* var. *purpurea*)
Quartz Creek rush (*Juncus effusus* 'Quartz Creek')
Ruby Silver monkeyflower (*Mimulus* 'Ruby Silver')
San Diego sedge (*Carex spissa*)

Sarah Lyman polypody fern
Polypodium californicum
'Sarah Lyman')
scarlet bugler (*Penstemon
centranthifolius*)
sedge (*Carex* species)
showy penstemon (*Penstemon
spectabilis*)
spreading gum plant (*Grindelia
stricta* var. *venulosa*)
Stoney Creek Idaho fescue (*Festuca
idahoensis* 'Stoney Creek')
Sulfer Yellow monkeyflower
(*Mimulus* 'Sulfer Yellow')
Wendy coral bells (*Heuchera*
'Wendy')
western columbine (*Aquilegia
formosa*)
Will Flemming wire grass (*Juncus*
'Will Flemming')
wire grass (*Juncus patens*)
wishbone bush (*Mirabilis
californica*)

GROUNDCOVERS
frogfruit (*Phyla nodiflora*)
Frosty Dawn California lilac
(*Ceanothus maritimus* 'Frosty
Dawn')
Joyce Coulter California lilac
(*Ceanothus* 'Joyce Coulter')

SUCCULENTS
Blue Flame agave (*Agave* 'Blue
Flame')
Catalina Island live-forever
(*Dudleya virens* ssp. *hassei*)
coast opuntia (*Opuntia prolifera*)
Frank Reinelt live-forever
(*Dudleya* 'Frank Reinelt')
live-forever (*Dudleya* species and
cultivars)

Parry beargrass (*Nolina parryi*)
Shaw's agave (*Agave shawii*)
White Sprite dudleya (*Dudleya
gnoma* 'White Sprite')

BULBS
soap plant (*Chlorogalum
pomeridianum* var. *divaricatum*)

VINES
pipestems (*Clematis lasiantha*)
Roger's Red grape (*Vitis* 'Roger's
Red')

ANNUALS
arroyo lupine (*Lupinus succulentus*)
baby blue eyes (*Nemophila
menziesii*)
bird's-eye gilia (*Gilia tricolor*)
California poppy (*Eschscholzia
californica*)
Canterbury bells (*Phacelia minor*)
chia (*Salvia columbariae*)
common madia (*Madia elegans*
ssp. *elegans*)
desert bluebells (*Phacelia
campanularia*)
farewell-to-spring (*Clarkia amoena*)
five spot (*Nemophila maculata*)
globe gilia (*Gilia capitata*)
goldfields (*Lasthenia glabrata*)
miniature lupine (*Lupinus bicolor*)
Montana de Oro wood strawberry
(*Fragaria vesca*)
mountain garland (*Clarkia
unguiculata*)
sunflower (*Helianthus annuus*)
tansy-leafed phacelia (*Phacelia
tanacetifolia*)
tidy-tips (*Layia platyglossa*)
winecup clarkia (*Clarkia purpurea*)
yellow lupine (*Lupinus microcarpus*
var. *densiflorus*)

APPENDIX C
WHERE TO SEE NATIVE PLANT
GARDENS IN SOUTHERN CALIFORNIA

THE FOLLOWING LIST includes long-established botanical gardens, arboretums, and nursery demonstration gardens that showcase native and low-water-use plants.

BOTANICAL GARDENS AND ARBORETA

Conejo Valley Botanic Garden
400 W. Gainsborough Road,
Thousand Oaks, CA 91358
(805) 494-7630
conejogarden.com
Highlights: collections of native plants, oak trees, and water-conserving plants

Descanso Gardens
1418 Descanso Drive, La Cañada Flintridge, CA 91011
(818) 952-4400;
descansogardens.org
Highlights: native plant section

Fullerton Arboretum
California State University Fullerton, Fullerton, CA 92634
(714) 733-3579
fullertonarboretum.org
Highlights: Mediterranean section with plants from coastal sage scrub and chaparral communities

Huntington Botanical Gardens
Frances and Sidney Brody
California Garden
1151 Oxford Road,
San Marino, CA 91108
(626) 405-2100
huntington.org/californiagarden/
Highlights: 6.5 acres of gardens with California native and dry-climate plants

Leaning Pine Arboretum
California Polytechnic State University, San Luis Obispo, CA 93405
(805) 756-2161
leaningpinearboretum.calpoly.edu
Highlights: five acres of Mediterranean-climate garden plants, including those native to California

The Living Desert Zoo and Gardens
Palo Verde Garden Center and Wortz Demonstration Garden
47900 Portola Avenue,
Palm Desert, CA 92260
(760) 346-5694; livingdesert.org
Highlights: desert plantings

Los Angeles County Arboretum and Botanic Garden
301 N. Baldwin Avenue,
Arcadia, CA 91007
(626) 821-3222; arboretum.org
Highlights: Sunset Demonstration Garden for California native plants; old stand of Engelmann oaks

Manhattan Beach Botanical Garden
1236 N. Peck Avenue,
Manhattan Beach, CA 90266
(310) 546-1354; manhattanbeach botanicalgarden.org
Highlights: drought-tolerant garden featuring low-water-use and California native plants

Mildred E. Mathias Botanical Garden
777 Tiverton Drive,
Los Angeles, CA 90095
(213) 825-3620; botgard.ucla.edu
Highlights: coastal sage scrub, Channel Islands and chaparral communities

Rancho Santa Ana Botanic Garden
1500 N. College Avenue,
Claremont, CA 91711
(909) 625-8767; rsabg.org
Highlights: largest botanical garden devoted to the collection, cultivation, study, and display of California native plants

San Diego Botanic Garden
(formerly Quail Botanical Garden)
230 Quail Gardens Drive,
Encinitas, CA 92024
(760) 436-3036; sdbgarden.org
Highlights: native plant and ethnobotanical garden; natural coastal habitat sections

San Luis Obispo Botanical Garden
3450 Dairy Creek Road,
San Luis Obispo, CA 93405
(805) 541-1400; slobg.org
Highlights: Mediterranean and native plants

Santa Barbara Botanic Garden
1212 Mission Canyon Road,
Santa Barbara, CA 93105
(805) 682-4726; sbbg.org
Highlights: fosters stewardship of the natural world with emphasis on California native plants

University of California Riverside Botanic Gardens
900 University Avenue,
Riverside, CA 92521
(951) 784-6962 or 787-4650
gardens.ucr.edu
Highlights: southwestern desert and Sierra foothills sections

NURSERY DEMONSTRATION GARDENS

Las Pilitas Nursery
8331 Nelson Way,
Escondido, CA 92026
(760) 749-5930

laspilitas.com/nurseries/escondido.htm
Highlights: demonstration garden, wi-fi available in the nursery area

Theodore Payne Foundation
10459 Tuxford Street,
Sunland, CA 91352
(818) 768-1802
theodorepayne.org
Highlights: demonstration garden
areas, a wildflower nature trail, and
natural canyon areas

Tree of Life Nursery
33201 Ortega Highway,
P.O. Box 635,
San Juan Capistrano, CA 92693
(949) 728-0685
californianativeplants.com
Highlights: retail bookstore, nursery
landscaped with native plants

APPENDIX D
WHERE TO GET CALIFORNIA NATIVE PLANTS IN SOUTHERN CALIFORNIA

THESE SOURCES FOR native plants include botanical gardens, wholesale and retail outlets in Southern California, and statewide sources for native seeds and bulbs through mail order.

BOTANICAL GARDENS, FOUNDATIONS, AND SOCIETIES

**California Native Plant Society
(Local Chapters)**
cnps.org
Notes: plant sales run by local
chapters

The Living Desert
47900 Portola Avenue,
Palm Desert, CA 92260
(760) 346-5694
livingdesert.org
Notes: Southwestern, native
California, and desert plants in
the Palo Verde Garden Center

Rancho Santa Ana Botanic Garden
1500 N. College Avenue,
Claremont, CA 91711
(909) 625-8767; rsabg.org
Notes: California natives in the
Grow Native Nursery; Fall Planting
Festival held the first weekend in
October

Santa Barbara Botanic Garden
1212 Mission Canyon Road,
Santa Barbara, CA 93105
(805) 682-4726; sbbg.org
Notes: spring and fall sales held
all year in the Garden Growers
Nursery

Theodore Payne Foundation
10459 Tuxford Street,
Sun Valley, CA 91352
(818) 768-1802
theodorepayne.org
Notes: nonprofit retail
California native plant nursery

University of California Riverside Botanic Gardens
900 University Avenue, Riverside,
CA 92521
(909) 784-6962; gardens.ucr.edu
Notes: Native plants included in the
fall plant sale

COMMERCIAL WHOLESALE AND RETAIL NATIVE PLANT NURSERIES

Back to Natives Nursery
Santiago Park Nature Reserve,
Santa Ana, CA 92706
(949) 509-4787
backtonatives.org/nursery

El Nativo Growers, Inc.
200 S. Peckham Road,
Azusa, CA 91702
(626) 969-8449
elnativogrowers.com

Las Pilitas Nursery
8331 Nelson Way,
Escondido, CA 92026
(760) 749-5930; laspilitas.com

Matilija Nursery
8225 Waters Road,
Moorpark, CA 93021
(805) 978-8760
matilijanursery.com

Mockingbird Nursery
1670 Jackson Street,
Riverside, CA 92504
(951) 780-3571
mockingbirdnursery.com

Moosa Creek Nursery California Native Plant Nursery
28435 Wilkes Road,
Valley Center, CA 92082
(760) 749-3216
moosacreeknursery.com

Native Sons Wholesale Nursery
379 W. El Campo Road,
Arroyo Grande, CA 93420
(805) 481-5996
nativeson.com

RECON Native Plants, Inc.
1755 Saturn Boulevard,
San Diego, CA 92154
(619) 423-2284
reconnativeplants.com

San Marcos Growers
125 S. San Marcos Road,
Santa Barbara, CA 93111
(805) 683-1561
smgrowers.com

Tarweed Nursery and Landscape
1307 Graynold Avenue,
Glendale, CA 91202
(open by appointment only)
(626) 705-8993
tarweednativeplants.com

Tree of Life Nursery
33201 Ortega Highway,
P.O. Box 635,
San Juan Capistrano, CA 92693
(949) 728-0685
californianativeplants.com

NATIVE SEEDS BY MAIL ORDER

Clyde Robin Seed Company
P.O. Box 2366,
Castro Valley, CA 94546
(510) 315-6720; clyderobin.com

Larner Seeds
P.O. Box 407, Bolinas, CA 94924
(415) 868-9407; larnerseeds.com

Hedgerow Farms
21905 County Road 88,
Winters, CA 95694
(530) 662-6847
hedgerowfarms.com

Moon Mountain Wildflowers
P.O. Box 725,
Carpinteria, CA 93014
(805) 684-2565

Plants of the Southwest
3095 Agua Fria Road,
Santa Fe, NM 87507
6680 4th Street NW,
Albuquerque, NM 87107
(800) 788-7333
plantsofthesouthwest.com

S&S Seed
P.O. Box 1275,
Carpinteria, CA 93014
(805) 684-0436
ssseeds.com

Seedhunt
P.O. Box 96,
Freedom, CA 95019
seedhunt.com

Sierra Seed Supply
358 Williams Valley Road,
Greenville, CA 95947
(530) 284-7926
sierraseedsupply.com

Theodore Payne Foundation
10459 Tuxford Street,
Sun Valley, CA 91352
(818) 768-1802
theodorepayne.org

NATIVE BULBS BY MAIL ORDER

**Bay View Gardens—
The Irises of Joe Ghio**
1201 Bay Street,
Santa Cruz, CA 95060
(831) 423-3656
Email: ghiobayview@surfnetusa
.com

Far West Bulb Farm
14499 Lower Colfax Road,
Grass Valley, CA 95945
(530) 272-4775
californianativebulbs.com

Telos Rare Bulbs
P.O. Box 4147,
Arcata, CA 95518
telosrarebulbs.com

Van Engelen Inc.
(John Scheepers, Inc.)
23 Tulip Drive,
P.O. Box 638,
Bantam, CT 06750
(860) 567-8734
vanengelen.com
johnscheepers.com

RESOURCES

PLANTS IN THE BOOK

alkali sacaton (*Sporobolus airoides*)

baby blue eyes (*Nemophila menziesii*)

Bee's Bliss sage (*Salvia* 'Bee's Bliss')

Betsy Clebsch Cleveland sage (*Salvia clevelandii* 'Betsy Clebsch')

bigleaf crownbeard (*Verbesina dissita*)

bird's-eye gilia (*Gilia tricolor*)

buckwheat (*Eriogonum*)

California buckwheat (*Eriogonum fasciculatum*)

California fuchsia (*Epilobium* [formerly *Zauschneria*])

California goldenrod (*Solidago velutina* ssp. *californica* [formerly *S. californica*])

California poppy (*Eschscholzia californica*)

California sagebrush (*Artemisia californica*)

Canyon Prince giant wild rye (*Elymus* [formerly *Leymus*] *condensatus* 'Canyon Prince')

Cleveland sage (*Salvia clevelandii*)

coast live oak (*Quercus agrifolia*)

coffeeberry (*Frangula* [formerly *Rhamnus*] *californica*)

common manzanita (*Arctostaphylos manzanita*)

creeping barberry (*Berberis* [formerly *Mahonia*] *aquifolium* var. *repens*)

David's Choice sandhill sagebrush (*Artemisia pycnocephala* 'David's Choice')

De La Mina lilac verbena (*Verbena lilacina* 'De La Mina')

deer grass (*Muhlenbergia rigens*)

desert four-o'clock (*Mirabilis multiflora* var. *pubescens*)

Desert Museum palo verde (*Parkinsonia* 'Desert Museum')

desert peach (*Prunus andersonii*)

farewell-to-spring (*Clarkia amoena*)

Frosty Blue California lilac (*Ceanothus* 'Frosty Blue')

Frosty Dawn California lilac (*Ceanothus maritimus* 'Frosty Dawn')

Genevieve coral bells (*Heuchera* 'Genevieve')

giant coreopsis (*Leptosyne* [formerly *Coreopsis*] *gigantea*)

globe gilia (*Gilia capitata*)

Golden Abundance barberry (*Berberis* [formerly *Mahonia*] 'Golden Abundance')

202

grand linanthus (*Leptosiphon* [formerly *Linanthus*] *grandiflorus*)

Howard McMinn manzanita (*Arctostaphylos* 'Howard McMinn')

hummingbird sage (*Salvia spathacea*)

live-forever (*Dudleya*)

manzanita (*Arctostaphylos*)

Margarita BOP penstemon (*Penstemon heterophyllus* 'Margarita BOP')

monkeyflower (*Mimulus*)

Pacific Coast Hybrid iris (*Iris*–PCH)

Palmer's mallow (*Abutilon palmeri*)

Pigeon Point coyote brush (*Baccharis pilularis* 'Pigeon Point')

Pozo Blue sage (*Salvia* 'Pozo Blue')

purple sage (*Salvia leucophylla*)

Ray Hartman California lilac (*Ceanothus* 'Ray Hartman')

Roger's Red grape (*Vitis* 'Roger's Red')

Russian River wild grape (*Vitis californica* 'Russian River')

sage (*Salvia*)

sagebrush (*Artemisia*)

Santa Catalina live-forever (*Dudleya virens* ssp. *hassei*)

seaside daisy (*Erigeron glaucus*)

Silver Carpet California aster (*Corethrogyne* [formerly *Lessingia*] *filaginifolia*)

sugar bush (*Rhus ovata*)

sulphur-flower buckwheat (*Eriogonum umbellatum*)

tansy-leafed phacelia (*Phacelia tanacetifolia*)

tidy-tips (*Layia platyglossa*)

toyon (*Heteromeles arbutifolia*)

valley oak (*Quercus lobata*)

W. R. seaside daisy (*Erigeron* 'W. R.')

Wendy coral bells (*Heuchera* 'Wendy')

western sycamore (*Platanus racemosa*)

white sage (*Salvia apiana*)

wild strawberry (*Fragaria*)

Winnifred Gilman Cleveland sage (*Salvia clevelandii* 'Winnifred Gilman')

wire grass (*Juncus*)

Yankee Point California lilac (*Ceanothus thyrsiflorus* var. *griseus* 'Yankee Point')

yellow lupine (*Lupinus microcarpus* var. *densiflorus*)

24   *Resources*

FURTHER READING

Allen, Laura. *The Waterwise Home: How to Conserve, Capture, and Reuse Water in Your Home and Landscape.* North Adams, MA: Storey Publishing, 2015. **Topics:** rainwater harvesting, water conservation, hardscape

Allen, Robert L., and Fred M. Roberts, Jr. *Wildflowers of Orange County and the Santa Ana Mountains.* Laguna Beach: Laguna Wilderness Press, 2013. **Topics:** wildflowers, plant identification, plant/insect interaction

Bakker, Elna S. *An Island Called California: An Ecological Introduction to Its Natural Communities.* Berkeley: UC Press, 1971. **Topics:** ecology, natural history

Bauer, Nancy. *The California Wildlife Habitat Garden.* Berkeley: UC Press, 2012. **Topic:** habitat gardening

Bornstein, Carol, David Fross, and Bart O'Brien. *California Native Plants for the Garden.* Los Olivos, CA: Cachuma Press, 2005. **Topics:** plant descriptions, plant lists

————. *Reimagining the California Lawn.* Los Olivos, CA: Cachuma Press, 2011. **Topics:** plant descriptions, lawn removal

Clebsch, Betsy. *The New Book of Salvias.* Portland, OR: Timber Press, 2003. **Topics:** salvia descriptions

Dallman, Peter R. *Plant Life in the World's Mediterranean Climates.* Berkeley: UC Press, 1988. **Topics:** natural history, Mediterranean plants

Dell, Owen. *Sustainable Landscaping for Dummies.* Hoboken, NJ: Wiley, 2009. **Topics:** landscaping, hardscape, irrigation

Emery, Dara. *Seed Propagation of Native California Plants.* Santa Barbara, CA: Santa Barbara Botanic Garden, 1988. **Topics:** seeds, propagation

Emery, Dara, and Jacqueline Broughton. *Native Plants for Southern California Gardens: Cultural and Environmental Requirements.* Leaflets of the Santa Barbara Botanic Garden, vol. 1, no. 12. Santa Barbara, CA: Santa Barbara Botanic Garden, 1969. **Topic:** plant lists

Francis, Mark, and Andreas Reimann. *The California Landscape Garden.* Berkeley: UC Press, 1999. **Topics:** ecology, culture, design, sustainability, habitat landscapes

Frankie, Gordon W., Robbin W. Thorp, Rollin E. Coville, and Barbara Ertter. *California Bees and Blooms*. Berkeley and Sacramento: Heyday and the California Native Plant Society, 2014. **Topics:** bees and plants, habitat gardening

Fross, David, and Dieter Wilken. *Ceanothus*. Portland, OR: Timber Press, 2006. **Topics:** planting, care, and descriptions of ceanothus

Hagen, Bruce W., Barrie D. Coate, and Keith Oldham. *Compatible Plants Under and Around Oaks*. Sacramento: California Oak Foundation, 1991. **Topic:** planting under oaks

Hannebaum, Leroy G. *Landscape Design: A Practical Approach*, 4th ed. Upper Saddle River, NJ: Prentice-Hall, 1997. **Topics:** landscape design principles, hardscape

Harlow, Nora, and Kristen Jakob, eds. *Wild Lilies, Irises, and Grasses*. Berkeley: UC Press, 2003. **Topics:** descriptions of grasses, irises, lilies

Hickman, James C., ed. *The Jepson Manual: Higher Plants of California*. Berkeley, CA: UC Press, 1993. **Topics:** natural history, habitats, plant descriptions

Irish, Mary F. "Desert Plants for Desert Gardens," in Rancho Santa Ana Botanic Garden Occasional Publications No. 2, *Out of the Wild, Into the Garden II*, edited by Bart C. O'Brien, Lorrae C. Fuentes, and Lydia F. Newcombe. Claremont, CA: Rancho Santa Ana Botanic Garden, 1997. **Topic:** desert plant lists

Keator, Glenn. *Complete Garden Guide to the Native Shrubs of California*. San Francisco: Chronicle, 1994. **Topic:** plant descriptions

Keator, Glenn, and Alrie Middlebrook. *Designing California Native Gardens*. Berkeley: UC Press, 2007. **Topics:** plant lists, plant communities, ecological gardening

Lancaster, Brad. *Rainwater Harvesting for Drylands and Beyond*. Tucson, AZ: Rainsource Press, 2014. **Topic:** rainwater harvesting

Landis, Betsey. *Southern California Native Plants for School Gardens*. Los Angeles: California Native Plant Society, 1999. **Topics:** plant descriptions, plant associations, habitat value, soils, butterfly gardens, ethnobotany

Lenz, Lee W. *Native Plants for California Gardens*. Claremont, CA: Rancho Santa Ana Botanic Garden, 1956. **Topic:** plant descriptions

Lenz, Lee W., and John Dourley. *California Native Trees and Shrubs*. Claremont, CA: Rancho Santa Ana Botanic Garden, 1981. **Topic:** plant descriptions

Louv, Richard. *Last Child in the Woods*. Chapel Hill, NC: Algonquin Books of Chapel Hill, 2008. **Topics:** children and nature

Lowry, Judith Larner. *Gardening with a Wild Heart*. Berkeley: UC Press, 1999. **Topics:** habitat, sustainability gardening

————. *The Landscaping Ideas of Jays*. Berkeley: UC Press, 2007. **Topics:** natural history of backyard restoration gardening

McMinn, Howard E. *An Illustrated Manual of California Shrubs*. San Francisco: J. W. Stacey, Inc., 1939. **Topics:** plant descriptions

O'Brien, Bart, Lorrae C. Fuentes, and Lydia F. Newcombe, eds. *Out of the Wild, Into the Garden*. Three volumes. Rancho Santa Ana Botanic Garden Occasional Publications, Nos. 1–3. Claremont, CA: Rancho Santa Ana Botanic Garden, 1997, 1999. **Topics:** plant descriptions, plant care, plant lists

O'Brien, Bart, Betsey Landis, and Ellen Mackey. *Care and Maintenance of Southern California Native Plant Gardens*. Los Angeles: Metropolitan Water District, 2006. **Topics:** plant care

O'Brien, Bart, and Bob Perry. *The California Classics Plant Palette*. Claremont, CA: Rancho Santa Ana Botanic Garden, 2002. **Topic:** plant lists by community

Pavlik, Bruce M., P. C. Muick, S. Johnson, and M. Popper. *Oaks of California*. Los Olivos and Sacramento, CA: Cacuma Press and the California Oak Foundation, 1991. **Topic:** California oaks

Perry, Bob. *Trees and Shrubs for Dry California Landscapes*. Claremont, CA: Land Design Publishing, 1989. **Topics:** plant descriptions, lists, and communities; planting advice; water conservation

————. *Landscape Plants for Western Regions*. Claremont, CA: Land Design Publishing, 1992. **Topics:** plant descriptions, lists, and communities; planting advice; water conservation

—————. *Landscape Plants for California Gardens.* Claremont, CA: Land Design Publishing, 2010. **Topics:** plant descriptions and lists, irrigation groups

Plaster, Edward J. *Soil Science and Management,* 3rd ed. Albany, NY: Delmar Publishers, 1997. **Topic:** soils

Popper, Helen. *California Native Gardening: A Month-by-Month Guide.* Berkeley: UC Press, 2012. **Topic:** garden care throughout the year

Rain Bird Sprinkler Manufacturing. *Landscape Irrigation Design Manual.* Rain Bird Sprinkler Manufacturing, 2000. Accessed online: rainbird .com/documents/turf/IrrigationDesignManual.pdf. **Topic:** irrigation design

Sauter, David. *Landscape Construction.* Albany, NY: Delmar Publishers, 2000. **Topic:** hardscape

Schmidt, Marjorie G. *Growing California Native Plants.* Berkeley: UC Press, 1980. **Topic:** plant descriptions

Schoenherr, Allan A. *A Natural History of California.* Berkeley: UC Press, 1992. **Topics:** ecology, natural history

Schumacher, Fred H. "The Use of the California Shrubs in the Garden Design," in *An Illustrated Manual of California Shrubs* by Howard E. McMinn. San Francisco: J. W. Stacey, Inc., 1934. **Topic:** plant lists

Smith, M. Nevin. *Native Treasures.* Berkeley: UC Press, 2006. **Topics:** plant descriptions, care, and propagation

Tallamy, Douglas W. *Bringing Nature Home.* Portland, OR: Timber Press, 2007. **Topics:** habitat, sustainability

Van Rensselaer, Maunsell. *Ceanothus, Part 1: Ceanothus for Gardens, Parks, and Roadsides.* Santa Barbara, CA: Santa Barbara Botanic Garden, 1942. **Topics:** ceanothus planting, care, and descriptions

INTERNET RESOURCES

Calflora	calflora.org
California Chaparral Institute	californiachaparral.com
California Flora Nursery	calfloranursery.com
California Invasive Plant Council	cal-ipc.org
California Native Plant Link Exchange	cnplx.info/index.html
California Native Plant Society	cnps.org
California Oaks	new.californiaoaks.org
CalPhotos: Plants	calphotos.berkeley.edu/flora
El Nativo Growers, Inc.	elnativogrowers.com/Natives.htm
Jepson Online Interchange for California Floristics	ucjeps.berkeley.edu/interchange
Las Pilitas Nursery	mynativeplants.com
Mountain States Wholesale Nursery	mswn.com
Native Sons	nativeson.com
Rancho Santa Ana Botanic Garden	rsabg.org
San Marcos Growers	smgrowers.com
Santa Barbara Botanic Garden	sbbg.org
Suncrest Nurseries, Inc.	suncrestnurseries.com
Theodore Payne Foundation	theodorepayne.org
Tree of Life Nursery	californianativeplants.com
University of California— Integrated Pest Management	ipm.ucdavis.edu
USDA Plants Database	plants.usda.gov
Yerba Buena Nursery	yerbabuenanursery.com

Elizabeth Eisenstein

BARBARA EISENSTEIN is a research associate and a former horticultural outreach coordinator at Rancho Santa Ana Botanic Garden in Claremont, California. She is the horticultural chair of the San Gabriel Mountains chapter of the California Native Plant Society and the founder and head of Friends of South Pasadena Nature Park.

ABOUT HEYDAY

Heyday is an independent, nonprofit publisher and unique cultural institution. We promote widespread awareness and celebration of California's many cultures, landscapes, and boundary-breaking ideas. Through our well-crafted books, public events, and innovative outreach programs we are building a vibrant community of readers, writers, and thinkers.

THANK YOU

It takes the collective effort of many to create a thriving literary culture. We are thankful to all the thoughtful people we have the privilege to engage with. Cheers to our writers, artists, editors, storytellers, designers, printers, bookstores, critics, cultural organizations, readers, and book lovers everywhere!

We are especially grateful for the generous funding we've received for our publications and programs during the past year from foundations and hundreds of individual donors. Major supporters include

Advocates for Indigenous California Language Survival; Anonymous (3); Judith and Phillip Auth; Carrie Avery and Jon Tigar; Judy Avery; Dr. Carol Baird and Alan Harper; Paul Bancroft III; Richard and Rickie Ann Baum; BayTree Fund; S. D. Bechtel, Jr. Foundation; Jean and Fred Berensmeier; Joan Berman and Philip Gerstner; Nancy Bertelsen; Barbara Boucke; Beatrice Bowles; Jamie and Philip Bowles; John Briscoe; David Brower Center; Lewis and Sheana Butler; Helen Cagampang; California Historical Society; California Rice Commission; California State Parks Foundation; California Wildlife Foundation/California Oaks; The Campbell Foundation; Joanne Campbell; Candelaria Fund; John and Nancy Cassidy Family Foundation; James and Margaret Chapin; Graham Chisholm; The Christensen Fund; Jon Christensen; Cynthia Clarke; Lawrence Crooks; Community Futures Collective; Lauren and Alan Dachs; Nik Dehejia; Topher Delaney; Chris Desser and Kirk Marckwald; Lokelani Devone and Annette Brand; J.K. Dineen; Frances Dinkelspiel and Gary Wayne; The Roy & Patricia Disney Family Foundation; Tim Disney; Doune Trust; The Durfee Foundation; Michael Eaton and Charity Kenyon; Endangered Habitats League; Marilee Enge and George Frost; Richard and Gretchen Evans; Megan Fletcher; Friends of the Roseville Public Library; Furthur Foundation; John Gage and Linda Schacht; Wallace Alexander Gerbode Foundation; Patrick Golden; Dr. Erica and Barry Goode; Wanda Lee Graves and Stephen Duscha; Walter & Elise Haas Fund; Coke and James Hallowell; Theresa Harlan; Cindy Heitzman; Carla Hills and Frank LaPena; Leanne Hinton and Gary Scott; Charles and Sandra Hobson; Nettie Hoge; Donna Ewald Huggins; Inlandia Institute; JiJi Foundation; Claudia Jurmain; Kalliopeia Foundation; Marty and Pamela Krasney; Guy Lampard and Suzanne Badenhoop; Thomas Lockard and Alix Marduel; David Loeb; Thomas J. Long Foundation; Judith Lowry-Croul and Brad Croul; Bryce and Jill Lundberg; Sam and Alfreda Maloof Foundation for Arts & Crafts; Manzanar History Association; Michael McCone; Nion McEvoy and Leslie Berriman; The Giles W. and Elise G. Mead Foundation; Moore Family Foundation; Michael Moratto and Kathleen Boone; Seeley W. Mudd Foundation; Karen and Thomas Mulvaney; Richard Nagler; National Wildlife Federation; Native Arts and Cultures Foundation; The Nature Conservancy; Nightingale Family Foundation; Steven Nightingale and Lucy Blake; Northern California Water Association; Panta Rhea Foundation; Julie and Will Parish; Ronald Parker; Pease Family Fund; Jean and Gary Pokorny; Jeannene Przyblyski; James and Caren Quay, in honor of Jim Houston; Steven Rasmussen and Felicia Woytak; Susan Raynes; Robin Ridder; Spreck Rosekrans and Isabella Salaverry; Alan Rosenus; The San Francisco Foundation; San Francisco Architectural Heritage; Toby and Sheila Schwartzburg; Mary Selkirk and Lee Ballance; Ron Shoop; The Stephen M. Silberstein Foundation; Ernest and June Siva; Stanley Smith Horticultural Trust; William Somerville; Carla Soracco and Donna Fong, in honor of Barbara Boucke; Radha Stern and Gary Maxworthy; Liz Sutherland; Roselyne Swig; Thendara Foundation; TomKat Charitable Trust; Jerry Tone and Martha Wyckoff; Sonia Torres; Michael and Shirley Traynor; The Roger J. and Madeleine Traynor Foundation; Lisa Van Cleef and Mark Gunson; Stevens Van Strum; Patricia Wakida; Marion Weber; Sylvia Wen and Mathew London; Valerie Whitworth and Michael Barbour; Cole Wilbur; Peter Wiley and Valerie Barth; The Dean Witter Foundation; and Yocha Dehe Wintun Nation.

GETTING INVOLVED
To learn more about our publications, events and other ways you can participate, please visit www.heydaybooks.com.